The Final

Cataclysm

Supernatural Signs

of the End Times

Volume 2

Josh Peck

D1733843

The Final Cataclysm: Supernatural Signs of the End Times
Josh Peck

Cover design by Jeffrey Mardis
ISBN: 9798312989243

6

Dedication

For my wife Christina and our five children: Jaklynn, Nathan, Adam, Lilly, and Anya.

Acknowledgments

Most of all, I'd like to thank my Lord and Savior, Jesus Christ, without whom I could do nothing. I'd also like to thank my incredible family: my wife, Christina, and our five children. I also must give a very big special thank you to Bob Ulrich, Gary Stearman, Mondo Gonzales, and everyone at Prophecy Watchers for the amazing support, encouragement, and friendship. You are all a blessing. Lastly, thank you all who decided to read this book. I pray it is informative, helpful, and edifying. Thank you all, take care, and God bless!

Introduction: Defending Against the Enemy

Now that we know a bit more about how our supernatural enemy might present themselves to the world, it would be a good idea for us to examine who and what these things actually are. The topic of spiritual warfare is an exceedingly important one for any Christian to learn. The more time goes by, the worse things get in the world. We are in a time called the "birth pangs" in the Bible. This term comes from Romans 8:20-22 of the New King James Version Bible, which reads...

"For the creation was subjected to futility, not willingly, but because of Him who subjected it in hope; because the creation itself also will be delivered from the bondage of corruption into the glorious liberty of the children of God. For

we know that the whole creation groans and labors with birth pangs together until now."

Jesus taught more about this in reference to the last days. In the King James Version Bible, John 16:20-22 reads...

"Verily, verily, I say unto you, That ye shall weep and lament, but the world shall rejoice: and ye shall be sorrowful, but your sorrow shall be turned into joy. A woman when she is in travail hath sorrow, because her hour is come: but as soon as she is delivered of the child, she remembereth no more the anguish, for joy that a man is born into the world. And ye now therefore have sorrow: but I will see you again, and your heart shall rejoice, and your joy no man taketh from you."

Jesus is speaking of His return to Earth. He states that the time before His return will be difficult and will keep getting worse with shorter periods of time in between hardships, just as a woman in labor. Then, He says when He does return, our hearts will rejoice to the point we won't remember the severity of our previous difficulties and that no one can take that joy from us. This is absolutely a wonderful promise from our Lord and savior.

Of course, Jesus does not expect us to just sit and wait around for His return. He did not leave us here to fend for ourselves. He did not leave us defenseless. The passage we examined is a message of hope but also a warning of the times we live in. God wants us to be prepared.

14

Part 3: Signs in the Occult: Demonic Doctrines and Practices

Chapter 11: Understanding Spiritual Warfare

The first step in preparedness is realizing the times we are living in. The Bible makes it very clear that we are living in the last days. Hebrews 1:1-2 states...

"God, who at sundry times and in divers manners spake in time past unto the fathers by the prophets, hath in these last days spoken unto us by his Son, whom he hath appointed heir of all things, by whom also he made the worlds;"

This passage shows that the "last days" began two thousand years ago during the time of Jesus Christ. That is why the passage says "these last day spoken unto us by his

Son". The Son is Jesus Christ, and the last days go from the time He walked the Earth to now. If it were not so, the Bible would not use the word "these". It would use words like "those" or "the future". This shows we are living in the last days today.

After we realize the days we are living in, we can begin to look in the Bible for descriptions and warnings about these days. There are many prophetic statements spoken of all throughout the Bible concerning our present time. There are descriptions as well as warnings. We can look to those prophetic passages to be prepared for what is ahead and what is already here.

Jesus spent a lot of time preparing His flock (also called the Church, meaning the full body of Jesus, Jew and Gentile, all believers) for the times we are currently living in. It is estimated that roughly one third of Jesus' teachings, and even the Bible as a whole, are prophetic in nature. Jesus Himself even seemed to allude to this. Luke 24:44 reads…

"And he said unto them, These are the words which I spake unto you, while I was yet with you, that all things must be

fulfilled, which were written in the law of Moses, and in the prophets, and in the psalms, concerning me."

Here, Jesus attributes one third of "all things" that "must be fulfilled which were written" to prophecy (or "the prophets" with the other two thirds being "the law of Moses" and "the psalms"). God devoting an entire third of the Bible directly to prophecy should give us cause to take notice.

The reason God spent so much time in the Bible writing about prophecy is simple; He loves us, cares about us, and wants us to overcome the evils we will have to face. God knows what will happen ahead of time. God is able to write history in advance (which is sometimes what Bible prophecy is referred to as in the modern Church). He uses that powerful ability to warn His children of dangers that lie ahead so we can be prepared and either avoid them completely, overcome them, or be able to gain strength and learning when they finally do hit.

The importance of Bible prophecy did not begin or end with Jesus' physical life on Earth. Many of the Old and New Testament prophetic writers put an importance on prophecy. Even God Himself spoke directly about the importance of true prophecy and the dangers of false prophecy. God spoke this through Moses in the Torah (the first five books of the Bible) Deuteronomy 13:1-5 states …

"If there arise among you a prophet, or a dreamer of dreams, and giveth thee a sign or a wonder, and the sign or the wonder come to pass, whereof he spake unto thee, saying, Let us go after other gods, which thou hast not known, and let us serve them; thou shalt not hearken unto the words of that prophet, or that dreamer of dreams: for the Lord your God proveth you, to know whether ye love the Lord your God with all your heart and with all your soul. Ye shall walk after the Lord your God, and fear him, and keep his commandments, and obey his voice, and ye shall serve him, and cleave unto him. And that prophet, or that dreamer of dreams, shall be put to death; because he hath spoken to turn you away from the Lord your God, which brought you out of the land of Egypt, and redeemed you out of the house of bondage, to thrust thee out of the way which the Lord thy God commanded thee to walk in. So shalt thou put the evil away from the midst of thee."

True prophecy was so important to God for the children of Israel that He commanded false prophets to be put to death.

That is how seriously He takes it when people misrepresent Him and/or twist around His words. The New Testament writer, Paul, fully understood the importance of prophecy. He speaks of this in great detail in chapter 14 of 1 Corinthians. For our purposes here, we will only look at a short selection of verses throughout this chapter. 1 Corinthians 14:1-6 reads…

"Follow after charity, and desire spiritual gifts, but rather that ye may prophesy. For he that speaketh in an unknown tongue speaketh not unto men, but unto God: for no man understandeth him; howbeit in the spirit he speaketh mysteries. But he that prophesieth speaketh unto men to edification, and exhortation, and comfort. He that speaketh in an unknown tongue edifieth himself; but he that prophesieth edifieth the church. I would that ye all spake with tongues but rather that ye prophesied: for greater is he that prophesieth than he that speaketh with tongues, except he interpret, that the church may receive edifying. Now, brethren, if I come unto you speaking with tongues, what shall I profit you, except I shall speak to you either by revelation, or by knowledge, or by prophesying, or by doctrine?"

Here, Paul explains the importance of the gift of prophecy by comparing it to another one of the Gifts of the Holy Spirit;

the gift of tongues. He explains the overall benefit to the entire Church that prophecy brings by comparing it to the personal benefit of speaking in tongues. He goes on with his explanation in 1 Corinthians 14:22-25, which reads…

"Wherefore tongues are for a sign, not to them that believe, but to them that believe not: but prophesying serveth not for them that believe not, but for them which believe. If therefore the whole church be come together into one place, and all speak with tongues, and there come in those that are unlearned, or unbelievers, will they not say that ye are mad? But if all prophesy, and there come in one that believeth not, or one unlearned, he is convinced of all, he is judged of all: and thus are the secrets of his heart made manifest; and so falling down on his face he will worship God, and report that God is in you of a truth."

Here, Paul is describing the benefit of prophecy over tongues in the case of witnessing to unbelievers. He uses an example of some unbelievers walking into a church; the unbelievers will think the congregation is crazy if they hear the entire church speaking in tongues, but the unbelievers will fall down and worship God if the members of the church reveal the secrets in the unbeliever's hearts. Prophecy can be used as solid proof that God is real when witnessing to an unbeliever. Paul even lays out specific instructions on how prophecy is supposed to be handled in a church environment. 1 Corinthians 14:29-33 states…

"Let the prophets speak two or three, and let the other judge. If any thing be revealed to another that sitteth by, let the first hold his peace. For ye may all prophesy one by one, that all may learn, and all may be comforted. And the spirits of the prophets are subject to the prophets. For God is not the author of confusion, but of peace, as in all churches of the saints."

It is clear that Paul understood the importance of prophecy.

Now that we understand the spiritual implication of Bible prophecy, we can begin to look at what the Bible has to say about the times we live in, our enemy, and the weapons at our disposal.

Time of War

As we looked at earlier, we are living in the last days. In many ways, the last days are a time of war. What that means for us Christians is we live in a time when we will be required to fight. While there are physical fights, battles, and wars that Christians will sometimes be involved in, we are mainly going to be focusing on spiritual warfare throughout the scope of this book.

The Bible has a lot to say about the time, setting, and players involved in the war we are engaged in. The enemy has done a real good job at convincing the Church to underestimate the severity of the war, even down to believing the war does not exist. The enemy believes if they can convince us there isn't a problem, we will not be trying to fix it, thereby giving our enemy free reign to do whatever they want in our lives and the world.

The Bible gives us many warnings and instructions concerning the last days and the war that rages around us. One such example can be found in 2 Timothy 3:1-7, which reads...

"This know also, that in the last days perilous times shall come. For men shall be lovers of their own selves, covetous, boasters, proud, blasphemers, disobedient to parents, unthankful, unholy, without natural affection, trucebreakers,

false accusers, incontinent, fierce, despisers of those that are good, traitors, heady, highminded, lovers of pleasures more than lovers of God; having a form of godliness, but denying the power thereof: from such turn away. For of this sort are they which creep into houses, and lead captive silly women laden with sins, led away with divers lusts, ever learning, and never able to come to the knowledge of the truth."

We are warned here of the characteristics that can be found in those who we should stay away from. We are even told of the kind of danger these people bring. It is saying these people are able to lead others astray to such an extent that they are never able to come to the truth. Without the truth, these people will never be able to come to repentance and find salvation in Jesus Christ. This is a specific warning concerning the days we live in about certain types of people that can lead us away from the truth. God warns us about this in the Bible because He does not want us to be deceived and fall away from Him. We should take these warnings very seriously.

When prophetically speaking of the last days, the Bible does not only give warnings. There are times when we are given promises of wonderful gifts from God. Such a prophecy was fulfilled when Peter and the apostles received the Holy Spirit. When this happened, Peter offered the onlookers of the event an explanation. In Acts 2:16-21, Peter said...

"But this is that which was spoken by the prophet Joel; and it shall come to pass in the last days, saith God, I will pour out of my Spirit upon all flesh: and your sons and your daughters shall prophesy, and your young men shall see visions, and your old men shall dream dreams: and on my servants and on my handmaidens I will pour out in those days of my Spirit; and they shall prophesy: and I will shew wonders in heaven above, and signs in the earth beneath; blood, and fire, and vapour of smoke: the sun shall be turned into darkness, and the moon into blood, before the great and notable day of the Lord come: and it shall come to pass, that whosoever shall call on the name of the Lord shall be saved."

Peter provided an explanation of the fulfillment of prophecy, future prophecy concerning the day of the Lord, and a promise that whoever calls upon the name of the Lord will be saved.

In his second epistle, Peter gives us even further insight into the last days. 2 Peter 3:3-7 reads...

"Knowing this first, that there shall come in the last days scoffers, walking after their own lusts, and saying, Where is the promise of his coming? for since the fathers fell asleep, all things continue as they were from the beginning of the creation. For this they willingly are ignorant of, that by the word of God the heavens were of old, and the earth standing out of the water and in the water: whereby the world that then was, being overflowed with water, perished: but the heavens and the earth, which are now, by the same word are kept in store, reserved unto fire against the day of judgment and perdition of ungodly men."

In this passage, Peter warns us of some of the deceptions that are going to run rampant through the world in the last days. He tells us that scoffers will ask where Jesus is and why He is taking so long to return to try and prove that all things are the same as they always were. He says these scoffers are "willingly ignorant", which means they are uninformed on purpose. This shows the information is available, but they choose to not look for it, not research it out, and not give it an honest chance; instead they stick with what they believe in and refuse to be open-minded and humble enough to look at other alternatives.

Peter even tells us what the scoffers are specifically willingly ignorant about. We can see this trend in the world nowadays. The world would rather believe in evolution instead of God and that we will never have to stand before God to answer for our sins after we die.

The truly appalling thing is nowadays we even have a few self-proclaimed Christians who match Peter's description of scoffers perfectly. We can match this back up with the previous passage of 2 Timothy 3:1-7. These are absolutely the people we must not fellowship with. We can't forget 2 Corinthians 6:14, which states...

"Be ye not unequally yoked together with unbelievers: for what fellowship hath righteousness with unrighteousness? And what communion hath light with darkness?"

Every day, more and more Christians are falling away from the Church and accepting these doctrines of devils over the truth of God. This is further discussed in 1 Timothy 4:1-3, which reads...

"Now the Spirit speaketh expressly, that in the latter times some shall depart from the faith, giving heed to seducing

spirits, and doctrines of devils; speaking lies in hypocrisy; having their conscience seared with a hot iron; forbidding to marry, and commanding to abstain from meats, which God hath created to be received with thanksgiving of them which believe and know the truth."

Again, we can see the prophetic importance and truthfulness in this passage. When referring to things such as listening to seducing spirits, speaking lies and hypocrisy, and forbidding to marry, it is obvious this is talking about the day in age we are presently in. We are living in the last days (or "latter times") and it is a time of war.

It is the will of God for the works of the devil to be destroyed. Ultimately, that was why Jesus was born; to undo all of the evil the devil and his followers have done throughout the Earth. 1 John 3:8 reads…

"He that committeth sin is of the devil; for the devil sinneth from the beginning. For this purpose the Son of God was manifested, that he might destroy the works of the devil."

We must fight beside Jesus in this war. To do nothing is where the enemy will use us best. If we are not fighting for

God, we are not fighting against Satan. Taking that stance allows Satan to come into our lives and the Church with free reign to do what he wants.

Satan is very successful at this. He knows all the ins and outs of the legalities he is bound by. He also has a lot of help from his followers. These followers are what the Church commonly refers to as "the enemy". Now that we understand the time of war we live in, we can examine our true enemy.

The Enemy

The Bible is very clear as to who our true enemy is. As Christians, we tend to follow the rest of the world in thinking that other people are the enemy. Some will look at false religions and say those who follow them are our enemy. Some will look at the vast number of murders of Christian and say the killers are our enemy. Some will even look to fellow brothers or sisters in Christ who have fallen back into a life of sin and say they are our enemy. Without knowing who our enemy is, we can never know who we are supposed to be fighting against or how we are supposed to be fighting. As with all else, we should first look to the Bible to define who our enemy truly is.

This is not really one of those topics that can be up to any sort of logical debate. The Bible is not vague here. We are told exactly who our true enemy really is. Ephesians 6:12 reads…

"For we wrestle not against flesh and blood, but against principalities, against powers, against the rulers of the darkness of this world, against spiritual wickedness in high places."

Paul tells us who are enemy is in great detail. For additional clarity, all we have to do is take these words back to the original Greek language.

First, Paul tells us that we do not "wrestle" against flesh and blood. The word "wrestle" comes from the Greek word "pala" and is defined as *"1) wrestling (a contest between two in which each endeavours to throw the other, and which is decided when the victor is able to hold his opponent down with his hand upon his neck) a) the term is transferred to the Christian's struggle with the power of evil."*[1] In essence, this is telling us that when an issue of any kind comes up and we decide to fight, we are not really fighting against the flesh and

---

[1] "Bible Search and Study Tools." Blue Letter Bible. Accessed February 24, 2025. https://www.blueletterbible.org/.

blood of the physical individual. In other words, people aren't the problem.

Satan is real good at keeping people focused on other people. This is especially true within the Church. The amount of animosity Christians will sometimes hold against his brother or sister in Christ is appalling. This is Satan's plan, to keep the focus off him by keeping us focused on each other. If we don't acknowledge a problem correctly, we have no hope of finding the correct remedy. If we go on thinking that other people are the problem, we will never find a lasting solution. That is why Satan wants to keep us pitted against each other.

If people aren't the problem, then what is? Who are we really fighting against? Paul answers that question by listing out the real culprits behind the issues that come up in life. Once again, going back to the Greek language will give us clear definitions of these individuals.

First, Paul says we are fighting against principalities. The word "principalities" comes from the Greek word "arche" meaning *"the first place, principality, rule, magistracy a) of angels and demons."* This is specifically referring to Satan himself. Being that the word "principalities" is plural, it would also be referring to the highest ranking fallen angels and/or demons directly under Satan. This is the same reference that is given in Romans 8:38-39, which reads…

"For I am persuaded, that neither death, nor life, nor angels, nor principalities, nor powers, nor things present, nor things to come, nor height, nor depth, nor any other creature, shall be able to separate us from the love of God, which is in Christ Jesus our Lord."

This entire construct of what Paul is talking about here can be compared to a type of government. Paul is describing the spiritual government on Earth controlled by Satan himself. The principalities (or sometimes referred to as "archons") are the highest branch of Satan's government containing his most powerful officials.

Next, Paul tells us that we fight against powers. The word "powers" comes from the Greek word "exousia" meaning *"the power of rule or government (the power of him whose will and commands must be submitted to by others and obeyed) a) universally 1) authority over mankind b) specifically 1) the power of judicial decisions 2) of authority to manage domestic affairs c) metonymically 1) a thing subject to authority or rule*

a) jurisdiction 2) one who possesses authority a) a ruler, a magistrate b) the leading and more powerful among created beings superior to man, spiritual potentates." This can be referring to those evil spirits that are under Satan and his highest officials. This can also be referring to the authority and abilities that Satan and his highest officials (or principalities) actually possess. By the wording of the passage, I say it could be either but is probably referring to both. This is the same word used when Satan was tempting Jesus. Luke 4:5-7 reads…

"And the devil, taking him up into an high mountain, shewed unto him all the kingdoms of the world in a moment of time. And the devil said unto him, All this power will I give thee, and the glory of them: for that is delivered unto me; and to whomsoever I will I give it. If thou therefore wilt worship me, all shall be thine."

In this passage, it is primarily speaking of the authority that Satan had. However, it is not specific as to what that authority was exercised through, so it is possible Satan could have been referring to the fallen angels and/or demons that were under him in his government. In both of these passages, the actual abilities of Satan and his cohorts are being discussed,

34

but it may not end there. If "powers" is also referring to evil spirits under Satan, that gives us new depth into the actual meaning of the passages.

First, in Ephesians 6:12, it gives us the definition of another branch of Satan's government that we need to watch out for and be prepared to fight against. Next, in Luke 4:5-7, we can see that Satan was actually offering Jesus his place as head of the satanic government, to be in charge and ruler over the "powers", and have spiritual control over the whole world. We can get a real look into Satan's desperation here. Satan was offering everything he legally had to give away, everything that was his, to try and entice Jesus into worshipping him. One act of worship, one sin, and Satan was willing to give up his entire kingdom. Of course, Satan knew by this point exactly who Jesus was and knew if he could get Him to fall, he would have legal right to remove God from His throne and set up his own satanic kingdom in Heaven, leaving his satanic spiritual government on Earth with Jesus. This really shows us how absolutely twisted Satan really is and how illogical his thinking can be. It is through that absurdity in Satan's way of doing things that makes him such a dangerous and powerful enemy.

Getting back to the branches of Satan's government, Paul tells us next that we fight against "the rulers of the darkness of this world". The word "rulers" comes from the Greek word "kosmokrator" meaning *"1) lord of the world, prince of this age a) the devil and his demons."* Quite simply, the rulers are Satan and those under them. There are no additional Bible references for this word because this is the only time it is used. To understand this word a bit more specifically, Paul gives us some further descriptions of exactly which rulers these are. They are the rulers of "the darkness of this world".

The word "darkness" comes from the Greek word "skotos" meaning *"of ignorance respecting divine things and human duties, and the accompanying ungodliness and immorality, together with their consequent misery in hell."* The same word is used in Luke 11:35, which states…

"Take heed therefore that the light which is in thee be not darkness."

This tells us these are the rulers who are directly involved with the ignorance of Godly things and human responsibilities, who promulgate ungodliness and immorality, and who already have some type of hellish misery. These rulers specifically make up the branch of the satanic government that is in charge of keeping people ignorant of the truth (such as the "willingly ignorant" people that Peter warned us about...it is because of these rulers that they remain willingly ignorant), keeping humans lazy and irresponsible, and making sure they remain ungodly and immoral. When we read over the description again, the "willingly ignorant" people Peter warned us about are the victims of these specific rulers; the rulers of the darkness of this world.

The word "world" comes from the Greek word "aion" and simply means *"period of time, age."* The same concept of "world" meaning "age" can be found in Matthew 13:40, which reads...

"As therefore the tares are gathered and burned in the fire; so shall it be in the end of this world."

This further solidifies the Biblical proof that the "willingly ignorant" people that Peter warned us about are victims of these specific rulers. Peter was talking about the last days, our day specifically. Paul was also talking about the rulers of darkness in this exact period of time as well. The rulers that are referred to in both passages are one in the same.

Lastly, Paul tells us that we fight against "spiritual wickedness in high places". The word "wickedness" comes from the Greek word "poneria" meaning *"evil purposes and desires."* Quite simply, we are talking about evil purposes and desires in a spiritual sense. This is referred to in Matthew 22:18, which reads…

"But Jesus perceived their wickedness, and said, Why tempt ye me, ye hypocrites?"

The word "high" comes from the Greek word "epouranios" meaning *"the heavenly regions 1) heaven itself, the abode of God and angels 2) the lower heavens, of the stars 3) the heavens, of the clouds."* This gives us the exact location of the satanic government. The actual evil purposes that come from the spiritual entities that have sided with Satan originate from the second heaven (the space between Earth and Heaven, where the fallen angels reside). This word is used in reference to another origin in 1 Corinthians 15:40, which states…

"There are also celestial bodies, and bodies terrestrial: but the glory of the celestial is one, and the glory of the terrestrial is another."

This is speaking of the celestial bodies of angels being of a heavenly origin.

Through all of that study, we are able to discover exactly who the true enemy is and what we as the Church need to be focused on. People aren't the problem. No human being could fit within any of those descriptions that Paul gave. We are speaking of evil and spiritual beings led by Satan himself.

These are the fallen angels and the demons that make up all the branches of Satan's spiritual government. This satanic government is incredibly powerful and is running the world today. What is interesting is Satan himself could fall into any of those descriptions. Satan could be a principality, power, ruler, or all three. The government of Satan could very well be the "spiritual wickedness in high places" that Paul specifically referenced.

When we take the Bible for the literal book of truth that it is, we can gain an incredible amount of insight concerning God's teachings and knowledge. From allowing the Bible to be our ultimate source of truth, we have discovered exactly who our true enemy is. Now we need to learn how to defend against them.

Weapons from God

God has given us a wide variety of weapons to use against the enemy. We have an entire arsenal of spiritual offensive and defensive weapons at our disposal. We have access to these weapons at all times. The only problem is we can't use what we don't acknowledge.

Satan knows this. He knows how incredibly powerful God's weapons are. Satan knows if we ever learn to use these weapons, the Church will be unstoppable and Satan will be left completely defenseless. Of course, Satan does not want that to happen, so he has spent a large portion of his time attacking the validity of the weapons within the Church. Satan knows it he can convince us the weapons aren't real, or convince us of a different interpretation, he will have his best chance at defeating us. He is trying to render us defenseless and, in many ways, he is succeeding.

Satan knows how to use our own pride against us. He uses our pride by convincing us that we are too smart to believe in things we cannot see, such as a spiritual war, weapons from God, and gifts of the Holy Spirit. The truth is that these things are very real and interact with us every day. Paul tells us that we have a whole armor of God that we should be putting on daily. Ephesians 6:10-11 reads…

"Finally, my brethren, be strong in the Lord, and in the power of his might. Put on the whole armour of God, that ye may be able to stand against the wiles of the devil."

Now that we know our true enemy, we need to understand the tools at our disposal. The enemy will bring about all sorts of different battles into our lives. The fortunate thing is that the enemy has no new tricks or devices. Satan might repackage his old tricks but at the core they are still the same tactics he used in the Garden of Eden. We know there is nothing that is truly new (Ecclesiastes 1:9). Time itself may be linear but the events in time are cyclical. In other words, history seems to repeat itself.

Since Satan and his angels have nothing truly new to use against us, only new ways to present their old devices, their tactics are predictable. The Bible gives us many examples to go by. If we want to know what the enemy is going to do in our lives, we only need to look at the accounts of spiritual battles in the Bible.

Though we call them "spiritual battles", that does not mean they will only be spiritual in effect. We call them "spiritual battles" because the battles are from a spiritual force working against us. Most times, they will manifest to us in physical ways. Paul wrote about his various battles in 2 Corinthians 11:24-28 which reads,

"Of the Jews five times received I forty stripes save one. Thrice was I beaten with rods, once I was stoned, thrice suffered shipwreck, a night and a day I have been in the deep; In journeyings often, in perils of waters, in perils of robbers, in perils by mine own countrymen, in perils by the heathen, in perils in the city, in perils in the wilderness, in perils in the sea, in perils among false brethren; In weariness and painfulness, in watchings often, in hunger and thirst, in fastings often, in cold and nakedness. Beside those things that are without, that which cometh upon me daily, the care of all the churches."

Spiritual battles almost always manifest in physical ways. In this passage, we are given a key to success no matter how bad any spiritual battle may get. After Paul listed out the various obstacles he had while trying to spread the gospel, he pointed out a solution. He made reference to "the care of all the churches". All of the churches that are giving Paul care would be included in the Body of Christ. Paul is telling us here, as well as many other places, that fellowship among Christians and having an active Church-life is a great way to combat the enemy. One of the most effective weapons we have against Satan is each other. There truly is strength in numbers.

Paul spoke extensively about overcoming spiritual battles on a personal level as well. We read in Ephesians 6:13-18...

"Wherefore take unto you the whole armour of God, that ye may be able to withstand in the evil day, and having done all, to stand. Stand therefore, having your loins girt about with truth, and having on the breastplate of righteousness; And your feet shod with the preparation of the gospel of peace; Above all, taking the shield of faith, wherewith ye shall be able to quench all the fiery darts of the wicked. And take the helmet of salvation, and the sword of the Spirit, which is the word of God: Praying always with all prayer and supplication in the Spirit, and watching thereunto with all perseverance and supplication for all saints."

These are our daily defensive and offensive weapons. We have truth, righteousness, the gospel of peace, faith, salvation, the Word of God, and prayer. Those seven things that make up our armor will ensure a victory over any battle if we utilize them properly.

We must be rooted in truth. This comes from God Himself through His Word. This is how we know the tactics of the enemy and the tools at his disposal. This is how we know what to do when any problem arises. We can't fall into the enemy's lies.

We must be actively practicing in righteousness. This means a right-standing with God. Our hearts have to be right with God. We can't let ourselves get caught up in continuing to live carnal and sinful lives.

We must have the preparation of the gospel of peace. We must be ready to share the gospel at any given time. We must also use the gospel for our own edification and growth by keeping it prepared in our minds. We must always be ready to proclaim the gospel and the promises of God. We cannot fall into any doctrines of devils.

We must have faith in God. We may not always know what He is doing or why but we need to trust Him. We have to have faith that He will make good on His promises. We need to have faith that the Bible is completely accurate and that everything God has said through His Word is true. We must not allow ourselves to fall into spiritual or physical doubt that comes in the form of fiery darts from the enemy.

We have to know and have assurance in our salvation. We can't allow ourselves to find comfort in false teachings of salvation, such as the many "works salvation" doctrines. We have to discover what true salvation is and allow God to lead us in it. We must allow ourselves to find true salvation through God's truth instead of the enemy's lies.

We have to know what's in our Bibles. We have to know and understand God's Word. This is our main offensive weapon. When Jesus was being tempted by Satan in the wilderness, He quoted scripture to fend him off. We know this was successful because every time Jesus quoted scripture, Satan had to leave for a while and come back again later. The Word of God is our main weapon against our enemy. We must not let the enemy keep us out of our Bibles.

Lastly, we need to know how to pray. We need to have an active prayer life for ourselves and our Christian brothers and sisters. We shouldn't only be asking God for things we need but we should also be giving Him praise and thanks for everything He has done for us. We must keep an open communication with our Great Commander. We must not let Satan intercept our prayers or interfere with our prayer life.

Those are the main weapons and armor God has given us against the enemy. If we can become informed and trained in those seven things, there is nothing the enemy can throw at us that we can't handle. We need to be united as a collective Church under Jesus Christ against the enemy. We must follow Paul's instruction. Ephesians 6:10-11 reads…

"Finally, my brethren, be strong in the Lord, and in the power of his might. Put on the whole armour of God, that ye may be able to stand against the wiles of the devil."

We have the power of God at our disposal; we just need to know how to use it. The power, strength, and might of God are in the form of His armor that He has provided for us. We will never be able to stand against our enemy without it.

We need to put on the whole armor of God daily and not just bits and pieces occasionally. We need to be prepared always, even when things are going good. We should not wait until we have a problem to utilize God's armor. We live in a battlefield with a constant war waging around us. We must always have on our armor. That is how we overcome any spiritual battle. The more practice and experience we can have in proper spiritual warfare, the stronger the entire Body of Christ will be.

To close out this section, though it is not mentioned specifically in Paul's list of the armor of God, we have another very powerful weapon at our disposal. This weapon is our tongue. Proverbs 18:21 states…

"Death and life are in the power of the tongue: and they that love it shall eat the fruit thereof."

We need to be aware of the things we say. We have the power to speak curses or blessings into our life even to the point of life and death. Now, this is not a "name it and claim it" kind of thing. We can't literally speak all sorts of material blessings into our lives. It's more about the consequence of how we use our words. Though there are many alternate weapons described throughout the Bible, I want to focus on this one because of the importance of its power.

Most of us don't really pay much attention to the kinds of things we say and the words we use in day to day life. This is not only merely about being optimistic or pessimistic. We can look at it in another way.

The absolute pinnacle of Satan's power is causing death. God's ultimate power is life. Proverbs 18:21 is telling us that death, life, and everything between are in the power of the tongue. The tongue's power is its ability to speak for us. Depending on what we speak, we can bring death or life into our lives or the lives of the people we are involved with. This is why prayer, praise, and worship are such strong tools in our lives.

When we pray, we are speaking directly to God. When we praise, we are giving God the glory He deserves. When we worship, we are expressing how much we love God. When we put these three things together, we can really get a sense of how powerful the tongue truly is. These are three things we can use to speak blessings into our lives in accordance with the will of God. It's not about getting new houses or cars.

Rather, it's all about worshipping God and developing our relationship with Him.

We have to watch out so as to not speak curses in our lives. Many times, when people become angry, they will say things they really don't mean. However, if we can learn to speak blessings against the curses, then we have learned a very powerful strategy in winning our personal battles. When someone speaks a curse of any form against us, we should either speak a blessing toward them personally and immediately, or later when we are away from that person. It is a difficult thing to put into practice but is incredibly powerful when we do.

I know that might sound foolish at first, but there is real validity there. When I first heard of this, I didn't really believe it either but I can say that it truly does work. Jesus said in Luke 6:27-28...

"But I say unto you which hear, Love your enemies, do good to them which hate you, Bless them that curse you, and pray for them which despitefully use you."

We have to consider the origin of the reason why a person would speak curses against us. They are being manipulated by the enemy. These people are just carriers of Satan's curses against us.

They may have been abused in their past or just be an angry person but the root cause will always lead back to Satan. This is why we have to look at people who curse others as cursed themselves. They are prisoners of war and not our true enemies. They are being used by Satan.

Our true enemy is Satan, including every evil spirit under him. Satan is just trying to use other people as his weapons and carriers of his tactics. If those people really knew what was going on and truly understood how they were being used, they would never speak curses against anybody. This is why Jesus told us the right way to handle those who curse us.

Jesus instructed us how to treat our human enemies in the right way, regardless how they are treating us. We must pray for them and speak blessings into their lives as well as our own. This will also bring forgiveness into our hearts and cast out hate, anger, pain, sorrow, and resentment. As the book of

Proverbs discloses to us, death and life truly are in the power of the tongue.

There we have a basic layout of the spiritual weapons and armor we have at our disposal. God, in His infinite mercy, grace, and love, has provided these weapons for us. If we utilize these weapons and walk in the armor daily, we will have a great advantage over our enemy.

Gifts from God

God has also given us many gifts. The source of these gifts is His Holy Spirit. After we are saved and baptized, God provides us with His Holy Spirit. There are nine specific gifts of the Holy Spirit listed in 1 Corinthians 12:8-10. Listed in order of mention, these gifts are...

- Wisdom
- Knowledge
- Faith
- Healing
- Miracles
- Prophecy
- Discerning of Spirits

- Tongues
- Interpretation of Tongues

For our purposes here, we will not be getting into an exhaustive study of these gifts. However, I will say here that these gifts are incredibly power and absolutely real. This Bible describes them that way and we must allow God to speak through His Word personally by studying the Bible for ourselves. If we are truly seeking after the truth, God will reveal it to us, but if we are only going to try to twist the Bible to fit around our preconceived beliefs, then we cannot expect Him to bless us in those regards. Having the correct knowledge is extremely important. Hosea 4:6 reads...

"My people are destroyed for lack of knowledge: because thou hast rejected knowledge, I will also reject thee, that thou shalt be no priest to me: seeing thou hast forgotten the law of thy God, I will also forget thy children."

God absolutely does promise us if we truly seek Him, He will reciprocate, but it is up to us to make the first move. James 4:8 reads...

"Draw nigh to God, and he will draw nigh to you. Cleanse your hands, ye sinners; and purify your hearts, ye double minded."

We are also told that, during our own personal battles and spiritual warfare, we can outlast the devil if we hold on. James 4:7 reads...

"Submit yourselves therefore to God. Resist the devil, and he will flee from you."

There is a stressed importance on the idea of obedience there. It is a common theme found all throughout the Bible. We must remain obedient to God. If we do, we will have a much closer walk with God. Ultimately, that will make us stronger. If we all would remain obedient to God and hold each other accountable, there would be absolutely nothing the enemy could do to us personally or the Church as a whole. Obedience to God is absolutely our strongest weapon against the enemy.

If we apply this knowledge, we will be able to have a closer walk with God and be able to keep more distance from the enemy. If we will follow God and His Word completely as our ultimate source of the only literal truth, we will be unstoppable and the devil will be absolutely defenseless. We must work together alongside of Jesus Christ to destroy the works of the enemy. We must do this for the good of the Kingdom, the Church, and ourselves.

Chapter 12: Mythology of CERN

Many people have probably heard the word "CERN," but perhaps not many know what it is, what it does, and why it exists. For those not familiar, CERN is the governing body of people who decide what to do with the LHC (Large Hadron Collider), the largest particle collider in the world, as well as other similar machines.[2]

For quite some time now, there has been suspicion circulating online whether or not CERN is an innocent institution or something more nefarious. While this question is

---

[2] "The Large Hadron Collider." CERN. Accessed February 19, 2025. https://home.cern/science/accelerators/large-hadron-collider.

far too large to cover in one chapter of one book, I thought it would be interesting to delve into some of the history surrounding CERN, going back to before the LHC was even built.

History of the Area

A large portion of CERN is found in a commune in eastern France called Saint-Genis-Pouilly.[3] This commune was actually identified as two separate towns. Before it was given the name Saint-Genis-Pouilly in 1887, the two towns were named Saint-Genix and Pouilly. Interestingly enough, Pouilly used to be a small Roman city by the name of Appolliacum.[4] Before dissecting the evidence surrounding the ancient city of Appolliacum, we should first delve into the history of Saint-Genis' namesake.

---

[3] Kunz, Tona. "An LHC Detector's Old Roman Roots." symmetry magazine, February 18, 2025. https://www.symmetrymagazine.org/article/may-2009/an-lhc-detectors-old-roman-roots?language_content_entity=und.

[4] CERN—looking for god particle, or opening portals of hell? | Christina Lin | The Times of Israel. Accessed February 19, 2025. https://blogs.timesofisrael.com/cern-looking-for-god-particle-or-opening-portals-of-hell/.

STATUE OF SAINT GINÉS DE LA JARA BY "LA ROLDANA"

The origin of the name of the town of Saint-Genis can be traced back to an individual who is surrounded by legends and mystery. It is generally believed the name Saint-Genis came from Saint Genest (also known as Genesius of Rome), a legendary Christian martyr.[5] The legend of Genesius of Rome states that Genesius, prior to his conversion, was once the leader of a theatrical troupe in Rome. In his plays, he would ridicule Christianity, especially certain rites. In one such performance, which was to be in front of an audience containing the Emperor Diocletian, Genesius was going to ridicule the sacrament of baptism.

The play began and Genesius took on his role of a person stricken ill. Two other actors asked him what was wrong and Genesius said he felt he had a weight on him that he wanted

[5] "St Genesius of Rome: Actor and Martyr." The fraternity of st genesius - actor and martyr. Accessed February 19, 2025. http://www.stgenesius.com/genesiusofrome.html.

removed. Next, two different actors, dressed as a priest and an exorcist, entered. When the actors asked what he wanted to alleviate his sickness, Genesius expressed he wanted to be baptized. It was shortly after this point in the play when things became very real for Genesius. He broke the fantasy of the play, claimed to see actual angels, and asked to be baptized onstage for real. This completely outraged Diocletian. Genesius persisted in his newfound faith, even to the point of torture and death by beheading.

Today, Genesius is regarded as the patron saint of actors, lawyers, barristers, clowns, comedians, converts, dancers, epileptics, musicians, printers, stenographers, and torture victims. His feast day is August 25. Coincidentally, August 25 is the same day Paris was liberated by the allies in 1944.[6]

Though recognized as a legend, there is a kernel of truth behind the story of Genesius of Rome. The very real Genesius of Arles is often combined with the legend of Genesius of Rome. Genesius of Arles was a notary who was

---

[6] "History Milestone: The Liberation of Paris." Origins. Accessed February 19, 2025. https://origins.osu.edu/milestones/the-liberation-of-paris-wwii.

martyred by Maximianus in the year AD 303.[7] He is the patron saint of notaries and secretaries, and his feast day is also August 25. It is said, while he was performing his secretarial duties, a decree of persecution against Christians was read out loud. Hearing this and becoming outraged, Genesius threw his tablets down to the magistrate's feet and fled. He was then captured and executed. Interestingly enough, the account of this mysterious individual does not end here. It is believed by scholars that Genesius of Arles is the same as the Spanish Saint Ginés de la Jara.

If true, this adds more depth to the story. The legend states that after Genesius of Arles was beheaded, he was buried in Arles, but angels transported his head to Cartagena. Another variation states that when Ginés was decapitated in France, he picked up his own head and threw it into the sea, which carried it to Murcia. These are thought as accounts to explain why stories of the same saint and the same cult are found in two different places. Also, the feast day of Saint Ginés de la Jara is August 25. The cult of Saint Ginés is thought to originate from the cults of the Islamic jinn, the Roman genius, or even with an ancient Carthaginian site dedicated to Ba'al.

---

[7] "Genesius of Arles." Oxford Reference. Accessed February 19, 2025. https://www.oxfordreference.com/display/10.1093/oi/authority.20110803095847499.

In Islamic belief, the jinn are beings made of smokeless fire that come from Djinnestan, another universe beyond our own. From a Christian perspective, these jinn might be viewed as fallen Seraphim and extradimensional in nature. The genius, in Roman mythology, is the "individual instance of a general divine nature that is present in every individual person, place, or thing." Lastly, the false god Baal-hamon was the supreme god of the Carthaginians. Baal-hamon was generally identified with the Greek god Chronos, the Roman god Saturn, and the Semitic god Dagon. Interestingly enough, Baal and Dagon are both mentioned in the Bible frequently.

The repetition of August 25 between the three representations of this mysterious individual certainly causes one to take note. The only common theme with this particular date seems to be, strangely enough, space exploration. On this date in 1981, the Voyager 2 spacecraft made its closest approach to Saturn.[8] On August 25, 1989, the Voyager 2 spacecraft made its closest approach to Neptune. On August 25, 2012, the Voyager 1 officially left our solar system and became the first man-made object to enter interstellar space. This apparent connection between the heavens and this

---

[8] "Voyager Fact Sheet - NASA Science." NASA, August 12, 2024. https://science.nasa.gov/mission/voyager/fact-sheet/.

mysterious individual of many names may have more parallels when we look into the namesake of the second town, Pouilly.

Pouilly was a small Roman city that likely took its name from the Latin Appolliacum. It is believed it was given that name out of dedication to the god Apollon. Apollon can be identified with the biblical Apollyon/Abaddon in the New Testament, the Greek god Apollo, and Nimrod of the Old Testament, who is sometimes known as "the man of many names." Just like Genesius (who could be called "the saint of many names"), Nimrod was also reported as being decapitated in the extrabiblical book of Jasher.[9]

Apollo was worshipped by the Romans as well as the Greeks. In Mauvières (Indre), a commune in central France, Apollo was equated with the Celtic god Atepomarus.[10] These two characters were combined to create Apollo Atepomarus, which can be translated as "Great Horseman" or "possessing

[9] "Book of Jasher, Chapter 27." Book of jasher, Chapter 27. Accessed February 19, 2025. https://sacred-texts.com/chr/apo/jasher/27.htm.

[10] Cartwright, Mark. "The Ancient Celtic Pantheon." World History Encyclopedia, February 19, 2025. https://www.worldhistory.org/article/1715/the-ancient-celtic-pantheon/.

a great horse."[11] In the Celtic belief, horses were closely related to the sun. The interesting thing to note is the connection between this idea of Apollo being associated with horses in France (where part of the LHC and CERN resides) and what the book of Revelation states about Abaddon:

And the shapes of the locusts were like unto horses prepared unto battle; and on their heads were as it were crowns like gold, and their faces were as the faces of men... And they had a king over them, which is the angel of the bottomless pit, whose name in the Hebrew tongue is Abaddon, but in the Greek tongue hath his name Apollyon. Revelation 9:7-11

Given these descriptions, is it possible CERN will have something to do with the opening of the bottomless pit described in Revelation 9? This is a possibility many researchers have looked into recently. With that prophecy in mind, we can look into other mythology and see more potential connections to CERN.

---

[11] "Apollo." Visit the main page. Accessed February 19, 2025. https://www.newworldencyclopedia.org/entry/Apollo.

CERN Found in Ancient Myths

Interestingly enough, the word "cern" can be found in ancient mythology. For example, in Dorset, England, there is the legend of the Cerne Abbas Giant, which is often associated with fertility.[12]

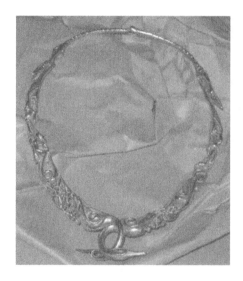

CELTIC BRONZE TORC

In Celtic mythology, the god Cernunnos is depicted as having antlers (or horns).[13] He is also shown with torcs around his neck and hanging from his antlers. Cernunnos is sometimes recognized as the god of nature or fertility. Torcs are large, metal neck rings that were once associated with nobility and high social status. The word "torc" comes from the

---

[12] "Cerne Giant: Dorset." National Trust. Accessed February 19, 2025. https://www.nationaltrust.org.uk/visit/dorset/cerne-giant.

[13] "Cernunnos." Encyclopædia Britannica. Accessed February 19, 2025. https://www.britannica.com/topic/Cernunnos.

Latin torque meaning "to spin."[14] It comes from this word because of the twisted shape many of the rings have.

THE SIGIL OF BAPHOMET

Because of the association with various creatures, Cernunnos is sometimes described by scholars as "lord of the animals" or "lord of the wild things." In biblical terminology, this could be understood as "lord of the beasts."

BAPHOMET, FROM ELIPHAS LEVI'S DOGME ET RITUEL DE LA HAUTE MAGIE, 1854

Cernunnos is also sometimes recognized as associated with sailors, commerce, and material wealth. Some may recognize this as a possible connection with Revelation 18.

Cernunnos has also been associated with Baphomet, an important deity in occultism. Baphomet is also synonymous with the symbol of the goat pentagram, also known as the

---

[14] "Torc - Wiktionary, The Free Dictionary." Wiktionary. Accessed February 19, 2025. https://en.wiktionary.org/wiki/torc.

"Sigil of Baphomet."

The original goat pentagram first appeared in the book "La Clef de la Magie Noire" by French occultist Stanislas de Guaita, in 1897.[15] It would later become synonymous with Baphomet, and is commonly referred to as the Sabbatic Goat. Samael is a figure in Talmudic lore and Lilith, a female demon in Jewish mythology.

The Hebrew letters at the five points of the pentagram spell out Leviathan, a mythic creature in Jewish lore. This symbol was later adapted by the Church of Satan in 1969 and officially named the Sigil of Baphomet.

The myth of Cernunnos is explained in further and more provocative detail in Italian witchcraft. Here, Cernunnos is known only as "Cern" and has a brother named Lupus. Cern is seen as the stag god while Lupus is seen as the wolf god.[16]

---

[15] Petersen, Jesper Aa. (2014). "Carnal, Chthonian, Complicated: The Matter of Modern Satanism". In Lewis, James R.; Petersen, Jesper Aa. (eds.). Controversial New Religions (2nd ed.). New York: Oxford University Press. p. 417. ISBN 978-0-19-515682-9.

[16] "Wolf Mythology: Rome & Italy. Divine Wolves among the Etruscans, Romans and across Ancient Italy (Hirpi Sorani, Suri, Aita, Calu, Aplu, Juno, Lupa Romana, Lupercalia." Homepage Ralph Häussler. Accessed February 19, 2025. https://ralphhaussler.weebly.com/wolf-mythology-italy.html.

It is said on the day of the spring equinox, Lupus was hit by a bolt of lightning shaped like an arrow while hunting a deer. Lupus then died and, on the next morning, rose from the underworld as the sun. Cern learned of his brother's death and became the "god of this world." The only thing left behind from the death of Lupus was his wolf skin, which was found in the forest by another hunter. It turns out the pelt had the magical power to transform men into wolves. The first man to wear this wolf pelt became a priest of Lupercus and founded the society of the Luperci.

We find a very interesting parallel to this story in the book of Jasher concerning Nimrod:

And Cush the son of Ham, the son of Noah, took a wife in those days in his old age, and she bare a son, and they called his name Nimrod, saying, At that time the sons of men again began to rebel and transgress against God, and the child grew up, and his father loved him exceedingly, for he was the son of his old age. And the garments of skin which God made for Adam and his wife, when they went out of the garden, were given to Cush. For after the death of Adam and his wife, the garments were given to Enoch, the son of Jared, and when Enoch was taken up to God, he gave them to

Methuselah, his son. And at the death of Methuselah, Noah took them and brought them to the ark, and they were with him until he went out of the ark. And in their going out, Ham stole those garments from Noah his father, and he took them and hid them from his brothers. And when Ham begat his first born Cush, he gave him the garments in secret, and they were with Cush many days. And Cush also concealed them from his sons and brothers, and when Cush had begotten Nimrod, he gave him those garments through his love for him, and Nimrod grew up, and when he was twenty years old he put on those garments. And Nimrod became strong when he put on the garments, and God gave him might and strength, and he was a mighty hunter in the earth, yea, he was a mighty hunter in the field, and he hunted the animals and he built altars, and he offered upon them the animals before the Lord. (Jasher 7:23–30)

Later we get the rest of the story:

And Nimrod dwelt in Shinar, and he reigned securely, and he fought with his enemies and he subdued them, and he prospered in all his battles. And all nations and tongues heard of his fame, and they gathered themselves to him, and they bowed down to the earth, and they brought him offerings, and he became their lord and king, and they all dwelt with him in the city at Shinar, and Nimrod reigned in the earth over all the sons of Noah, and they were all under his power and counsel. And all the earth was of one tongue and words of union, but Nimrod did not go in the ways of the Lord, and he was more wicked than all the men that were before him, from the days of the flood until those days. (Jasher 7:44–46)

We can see how Nimrod could be identified with Cern as the god of this world. In fact, Satan himself could be identified with Cern according to 2 Corinthians 4:4. Nimrod may also be identified with the first person who put on Lupus' pelts and became the priest of Lupercus. There are many ways to make connections and assign biblical identities to various myths surrounding Cern.

CERN's Modern History

Before CERN was a laboratory, it was a council whose purpose was to build the laboratory.[17] In 1952, the European Council for Nuclear Research was established by twelve European governments. The acronym "CERN" originally came

---

[17] "This History of CERN Timeline." The history of CERN. Accessed February 19, 2025. https://timeline.web.cern.ch/timeline-header/89.

from the French Conseil Européen pour la Recherche Nucléaire. In 1954, after the council was dissolved, the name changed to Organisation Européenne pour la Recherche Nucléaire, which translates to "European Organization for Nuclear Research." Former director of CERN, Lew Kowarski, stated that the acronym could have changed to OERN, but it was actually Werner Heisenberg (the famous physicist responsible for developing Heisenberg's Uncertainty Principle) who suggested the acronym should remain as CERN.[18]

CERN has had a number of achievements.[19] In 1973, weak neutral currents were discovered, which led to the discovery of the W and Z bosons (the elementary particles responsible for mediating the weak interaction) in 1983. The discovery of the W and Z bosons was a major breakthrough for what is now known as the Standard Model of particle physics. The W and Z bosons are still among the most exciting discoveries to date.

---

[18] Studies in CERN history. Accessed February 19, 2025. https://cds.cern.ch/record/162210/files/CERN-CHS-14.pdf.

[19] "This History of CERN Timeline." The history of CERN. Accessed February 19, 2025. https://timeline.web.cern.ch/timeline-header/89.

In 1995, the first creation of antihydrogen (antimatter counterpart to hydrogen) atoms occurred in what is known as the PS210 experiment. A normal hydrogen atom is made of an electron and proton (subatomic particles), however an antihydrogen atom is made of a positron and antiproton (antimatter counterparts to the electron and proton). In 2010, 38 atoms of antihydrogen were isolated. Antihydrogen was then able to be maintained without decaying for fifteen minutes in 2011. It is the hope of scientists that, by studying antimatter, they might discover the answer to what is known as the baryon asymmetry problem, which basically asks the question of why there is more matter than antimatter in the universe.

Conclusion

Does knowing the history and mythology surrounding CERN tell us definitively if there is something nefarious happening behind the scenes? Not exactly, but we do see some hints here and there. Of course, history isn't the only thing we can look at. In the next chapter, we will go through some of the more popular modern conspiracy claims surrounding CERN and we will see, one by one, if they hold any legitimacy. By going through all this information, bit by bit, maybe we can determine what's really going on with CERN.

Chapter 13: Occultism of CERN

For some time now, ideas about possible occult connections with CERN have been presented on various internet blogs and opinion columns. In this chapter, we will examine some of these claims to see if any legitimate connections can be made. What is presented here is a small percentage of the total evidence available. It is important to view these claims with an open mind; we should not accept these claims blindly, nor should we dismiss them without reviewing all of the evidence.

Statue of Destruction

Since its unveiling in 2004, CERN's statue of the dancing Shiva has caused quite a bit of controversy among Christians, especially in recent years.[20] Many look at the mythology of Shiva and the Nataraja dance and question the true motives of CERN. Is this statue meant merely as a piece of art or, as some claim, a foretelling of future destruction?

STATUE OF SHIVA ENGAGING IN THE NATARAJA DANCE AT CERN IN GENEVA, SWITZERLAND

The mythology behind this statue is certainly dramatic. Shiva is one of the main deities of Hinduism.[21] He is part of the Trimurti, the Hindu trinity. Shiva is known as "The

---

[20] "Lord Shiva Statue Unveiled." CERN Document Server, June 24, 2004. https://cds.cern.ch/record/745737?ln=en.

[21] "Shiva." Encyclopædia Britannica, January 31, 2025. https://www.britannica.com/topic/Shiva.

Destroyer" or "The Transformer" within the trinity. One depiction of Shiva is known as Nataraja, meaning "Lord of the Dance."[22] This is the depiction that embodies the statue at CERN.

The Nataraja depiction shows Shiva as the cosmic dancer who performs a divine dance to destroy a weary universe. Shiva does this in order to make preparations for the god Brahma to start the creation process. The statue shows Shiva in the middle of a circle of flames with his left leg raised and balancing over the demonic dwarf Apasmara who represents ignorance.[23]

Apasmara, in Hindu mythology, is a demon that cannot be killed. Hinduism teaches a balance between ignorance and knowledge, and to kill Apasmara would be to throw off the balance. This would mean knowledge would be attained without effort or hard work, thereby rendering it meaningless. Since Apasmara cannot be killed, Shiva uses his right foot to

---

[22] "Shiva as Lord of Dance (Nataraja): Indian (Tamil Nadu): Chola Period (880–1279)." The Metropolitan Museum of Art. Accessed February 19, 2025. https://www.metmuseum.org/art/collection/search/39328.

[23] "Apasmara Purusha." MAP Academy, November 29, 2024. https://mapacademy.io/glossary/apasmara-purusha/.

crush and subdue Apasmara during the Nataraja dance. It is believed that Shiva remains in the Nataraja form to forever subdue Apasmara.

The statue of Shiva at CERN contains an inscription of a quote by physicist Fritjof Capra, which states:

Hundreds of years ago, Indian artists created visual images of dancing Shivas in a beautiful series of bronzes. In our time, physicists have used the most advanced technology to portray the patterns of the cosmic dance. The metaphor of the cosmic dance thus unifies ancient mythology, religious art and modern physics.[24]

Shockingly, there is more to be read on the statue that claims Shiva as the most superior god of all religions. From the website of Fritjof Capra:

A special plaque next to the Shiva statue at CERN explains the significance of the metaphor of Shiva's cosmic dance with several quotations from The Tao of Physics. Here is the text of the plaque:

---

[24] "Lord Shiva Statue Unveiled." CERN Document Server, June 24, 2004. https://cds.cern.ch/record/745737?ln=en.

"Ananda K. Coomaraswamy, seeing beyond the unsurpassed rhythm, beauty, power and grace of the Nataraja, once wrote of it 'It is the clearest image of the activity of God which any art or religion can boast of.'"[25]

More recently, Fritjof Capra explained that "modern physics has shown that the rhythm of creation and destruction is not only manifest in the turn of the seasons and in the birth and death of all living creatures, but is also the very essence of inorganic matter," and that "for the modern physicists, then, Shiva's dance is the dance of subatomic matter."[26]

Once again, it is indeed as Capra concluded:

"Hundreds of years ago, Indian artists created visual images of dancing Shivas in a beautiful series of bronzes. In our time, physicists have used the most advanced technology to portray the patterns of the cosmic dance. The metaphor of

---

[25] Fritjof Capra. Accessed February 19, 2025. https://www.fritjofcapra.net/.

[26] "Shiva's Cosmic Dance at CERN." Fritjof Capra, June 20, 2004. https://www.fritjofcapra.net/shivas-cosmic-dance-at-cern/.

the cosmic dance thus unifies ancient mythology, religious art and modern physics. "[27]

Given the mythology behind the statue and the type of scientific pioneering CERN represents, it has caused many to wonder if there is a deeper meaning. Some have even gone as far as to claim Apasmara represents the church or the true God, Shiva represents Satan, the circle of flame represents a spiritual portal, and Shiva represents Satan traveling though the portal to destroy the church, subdue God, and take over the world. There are those who believe CERN and the LHC will be instrumental in this process.

Logo of the Beast

CERN'S OFFICIAL LOGO

Just as with the statue of Shiva, the logo of CERN has caused an equal amount of controversy. If turned upside down, the CERN logo resembles three sixes, which some claim is a clear sign of the biblical mark of the beast from the book of Revelation. This also resembles a hand

[27] Fritjof Capra. Accessed February 19, 2025. https://www.fritjofcapra.net/.

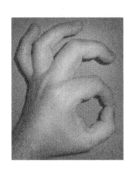

**HAND GESTURE
SHOWING 666**

gesture that is thought to signify the three sixes of the mark of the beast. Most times, this hand gesture is shown over an individual's right eye, signifying the "all-seeing

**THREE SIXES
(SIGNIFIED IN BLACK)
IN CERN'S LOGO**

eye" of the Illuminati and Freemasonry. There are some who interpret the CERN acronym in the middle of the three sixes as representing the eye.

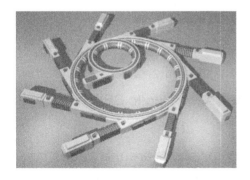

**SYNCHROTRON SOLEIL
PARTICLE ACCELERATOR
DIAGRAM**

Most people outside of conspiratorial research often deduce CERN's logo as representing nothing else but the design of synchrotron particle accelerators. It is even said that this was to be the original design for the logo, but it looked too much like a black hole. In my humble opinion, the symbol of the logo appears to be just a coincidence, but as it stands today, opinions are split as to whether we have a massive coincidence or a massive conspiracy.

CERN's World Wide Web

One of the more interesting and little-known facts about CERN is that the World Wide Web was actually created there.[28] The World Wide Web began as a project at CERN called ENQUIRE by Tim Berners-Lee in 1989 and Robert Cailliau in 1990. The project was originally intended as a way for researchers to share information. The very first website was activated in 1991. On April 30, 1993, CERN announced the World Wide Web would be available for everyone.

It is important to note that there is a difference between the World Wide Web and the Internet. According to BBC:

"The world wide web, or web for short, are the pages you see when you're at a device and you're online. But the internet is the network of connected computers that the web works on,

---

[28] "Where the Web Was Born." CERN. Accessed February 19, 2025. https://home.cern/science/computing/where-web-was-born#:~:text=Tim%20Berners%2DLee%2C%20a%20British,and%20institutes%20around%20the%20world.

as well as what emails and files travel across. Think of the internet as the roads that connect towns and cities together."[29]

The invention of the World Wide Web at CERN is of great importance to those who connect CERN with the mark of the beast of Revelation:

And he causeth all, both small and great, rich and poor, free and bond, to receive a mark in their right hand, or in their foreheads: And that no man might buy or sell, save he that had the mark, or the name of the beast, or the number of his name. Here is wisdom. Let him that hath understanding count the number of the beast: for it is the number of a man; and his number is Six hundred threescore and six. (Revelation 13:16–18)

One point that is brought up is how much of the world's buying and selling takes place on the Internet, but a more specific clue is given in the actual number 666.

---

[29] "What's the Difference between the Internet and the World Wide Web?" BBC Newsround. Accessed February 19, 2025. https://www.bbc.co.uk/newsround/av/47523993.

The letters of the Greek and Hebrew alphabets also represent numbers.[30] If you were to take three sixes and translate them through the Hebrew alphabet, you would be left with three of the letter vav. The Hebrew letter vav can translate to the English letter "w." Three sixes in Hebrew would equate to three w's in English. This would appear as "www," which, in our modern era, is recognized as standing for "World Wide Web."

This has been a semi-popular theory in Christian eschatology for a few years now. However, as some have pointed out, it has its problems as well. These arguments are presented here only in fairness to the reader and not to advocate one side over another.

First, and probably most obvious, is the text in question was written in Greek and not Hebrew. That alone doesn't discount the theory, since most of the Bible is written in Hebrew and those who wrote it spoke Hebrew, but it can hardly be used to support it, either. Another contention is the fact that the text states "Let him that hath understanding count the number of the beast: for it is the number of a man."

---

[30] Ratzabi, Hila. "What Is Gematria?" My Jewish Learning, March 25, 2024. https://www.myjewishlearning.com/article/gematria/.

Obviously, the Internet is not a man; it is something that was invented by man. Also, the text mentions, "six hundred threescore and six." This is exactly 666. If we were to add the three vavs of Hebrew, we would be left with the number 18. Therefore, it is believed the actual number of the beast will add up to 666 and will not be merely three individual sixes. After all, the text does not say the number of the beast will be "six and six and six."

There are, of course, a few more arguments against the 666/www connection. What is presented here are only a few. As stated earlier, it is important to view issues from all angles to make an informed decision as to what we will personally believe. It is also incredibly important to stay true to the text in question, at least as much as possible given the limited information available and our limited understanding.

The Toes of Prophecy

There is an idea that CERN may fit into biblical prophecy through some of its member states. In 1953, the CERN convention was signed by twelve original founding member states: Belgium, Denmark, France, the Federal Republic of Germany, Greece, Italy, the Netherlands, Norway, Sweden,

Switzerland, the United Kingdom, and Yugoslavia.[31] Since that time, many more member states have been added. All current member states are European, except for Israel, which was added in 2014.

One interpretation of Bible prophecy states that the Roman Empire will be revived through the European Union. This view comes from an interpretation of a passage in the book of Daniel:

After this I saw in the night visions, and behold a fourth beast, dreadful and terrible, and strong exceedingly; and it had great iron teeth: it devoured and brake in pieces, and stamped the residue with the feet of it: and it was diverse from all the beasts that were before it; and it had ten horns. I considered the horns, and, behold, there came up among them another little horn, before whom there were three of the first horns plucked up by the roots: and, behold, in this horn were eyes like the eyes of man, and a mouth speaking great things. (Daniel 7:7–8)

---

[31] "Member States." CERN. Accessed February 19, 2025. https://home.cern/about/who-we-are/our-governance/member-states.

This is explained in further detail later in the book of Daniel:

Thus he said, The fourth beast shall be the fourth kingdom upon earth, which shall be diverse from all kingdoms, and shall devour the whole earth, and shall tread it down, and break it in pieces. And the ten horns out of this kingdom are ten kings that shall arise: and another shall rise after them; and he shall be diverse from the first, and he shall subdue three kings. (Daniel 7:23–24)

The book of Revelation comments on this point as well:

And the ten horns which thou sawest are ten kings, which have received no kingdom as yet; but receive power as kings one hour with the beast. These have one mind, and shall give their power and strength unto the beast. (Revelation 17:12–13)

The idea here is that the fourth beast of Daniel represents the revived Roman Empire and the ten kings represent the kings of its member nations. The little horn, generally viewed as the Antichrist, rises up and takes control of three of those nations by conquering their kings. Thus, the Antichrist will control the entire Empire, and through it, the world.

Part of this interpretation also comes from another section in the book of Daniel:

Thou, O king, sawest, and behold a great image. This great image, whose brightness was excellent, stood before thee; and the form thereof was terrible. This image's head was of fine gold, his breast and his arms of silver, his belly and his thighs of brass, his legs of iron, his feet part of iron and part of clay. Thou sawest till that a stone was cut out without hands, which smote the image upon his feet that were of iron and clay, and brake them to pieces. Then was the iron, the clay, the brass, the silver, and the gold, broken to pieces together, and became like the chaff of the summer threshingfloors; and the wind carried them away, that no place was found for them: and the stone that smote the image became a great mountain, and filled the whole earth. This is the dream; and we will tell the interpretation thereof before the king. Thou, O king, art a king of kings: for the God of heaven hath given thee a kingdom, power, and strength, and glory. And wheresoever the children of men dwell, the beasts of the field and the fowls of the heaven hath he given into thine hand, and hath made thee ruler over them all. Thou art this head of gold. And after thee shall arise another kingdom inferior to thee, and another third kingdom of brass, which shall bear rule over all the earth.

And the fourth kingdom shall be strong as iron: forasmuch as iron breaketh in pieces and subdueth all things: and as iron that breaketh all these, shall it break in pieces and bruise. And whereas thou sawest the feet and toes, part of potters' clay, and part of iron, the kingdom shall be divided; but there shall be in it of the strength of the iron, forasmuch as thou sawest the iron mixed with miry clay. And as the toes of the feet were part of iron, and part of clay, so the kingdom shall be partly strong, and partly broken. And whereas thou sawest iron mixed with miry clay, they shall mingle themselves with the seed of men: but they shall not cleave one to another, even as iron is not mixed with clay. And in the days of these kings shall the God of heaven set up a kingdom, which shall never be destroyed: and the kingdom shall not be left to other people, but it shall break in pieces and consume all these kingdoms, and it shall stand for ever. Forasmuch as thou sawest that the stone was cut out of the mountain without hands, and that it brake in pieces the iron, the brass, the clay, the silver, and the gold; the great God hath made known to the king what shall come to pass hereafter: and the dream is certain, and the interpretation thereof sure. (Daniel 2:31–45)

There is obviously a lot that can be examined from this passage, but for our purposes here, we only need to view the highlights.

The interpretation we are looking at here generally views the prophesied kingdoms as such:

- Head of gold—Babylon (605–539 BC)
- Arms of silver—Medo-Persia (539–330 BC)
- Thighs of brass—Greece (330–63 BC)
- Legs of iron—Rome (63 BC–AD 1453)
- Feet of clay and iron—Revived Roman Empire

In this interpretation, the ten toes represent the ten nations spoken of earlier. Of course, there are certain problems with this interpretation. Most notably, there are far more than ten nations in the European Union today. As of today, it is comprised of twenty-eight states. Of course, there is always the possibility that some of these nations will be removed or come together in a way that will equate to ten once again, though this might be a bit of a reach.

The connection to CERN comes from its member states. The member states of CERN and the European Union are much of the same. However, due to this, the same problem arises. There are more than ten member states of CERN. Even if we only count founding member states, we still have twelve. Of course, just as with any problems of any interpretation of prophecy, there are ways around this as well. In considering these possibilities, the best bet is to treat them for what they are: possibilities. It never hurts to research them out to the fullest we currently can, then file them away for later. Things may change in the future to make this a more viable possibility, or they may not. Either way, only time will tell if we can fully accept or discount these interpretations.

Conclusion

I believe what is presented here is reason enough to show why we can't believe everything we read online. That said, just because something is found online doesn't necessarily mean it isn't true. As with all matters, it is important for us to take each claim on its own, weigh it against the available evidence, and make an informed decision as to what we will believe. Most importantly, if there isn't enough information to make a legitimate claim, then the best thing we can learn to say is "I don't know." Of course, when in doubt, it is best to consult the Bible on any applicable matters. Let's see if we can find CERN in other areas of Bible prophecy.

Chapter 14: CERN in Bible Prophecy

The graviton is possibly one of the strangest theoretical particles ever hypothesized. Gravitons have never been directly observed, however, physicists are confident in their existence due to the presence of the gravitational field.[32] It is possible a soon discovery might take place by means of particle colliders, such as the LHC at CERN.

Gravitons are the particles responsible for gravity. Gravity in itself is still a mystery in many respects, but due to scientific advancements, the world may not be far off from the holy grail

---

[32] "Will Physics Ever Prove That Gravitons Are Real?" Big Think, January 9, 2025. https://bigthink.com/hard-science/will-physics-ever-prove-that-gravitons-are-real/.

of physics: definitive proof the graviton actually exists and the means to study its properties.

What makes the graviton especially interesting is its apparent ability to flow free between dimensions.[33] Among other potential discoveries, the graviton is at the top of the LHC's to-do list.[34]

The idea is not always to look for the graviton itself, but to look for a gap where particles should be after a collision. The two particle detectors of the LHC (CMS and ATLAS) are able to show us the aftermath of a particle collision. As in any collision, debris is thrown out and distributed fairly evenly. If, however, the detector shows a gap where debris (or new and exotic particles) should be, that could be evidence they have escaped into a higher dimension.

There is an idea that gravitons can be used as a way to communicate with beings of higher dimensions. This may

---

[33] Tuttle, Kelen. "The Search for Extra Dimensions." symmetry magazine, February 18, 2025. https://www.symmetrymagazine.org/article/december-2005january-2006/search-extra-dimensions/.

[34] "Extra Dimensions, Gravitons, and Tiny Black Holes." CERN. Accessed February 19, 2025. https://home.cern/science/physics/extra-dimensions-gravitons-and-tiny-black-holes.

sound like the stuff of popular science fiction, but physicists today are seriously considering this possibility.[35] If gravitons are discovered and used as a way to communicate with beings of higher dimensions or parallel universes, this might be what tells the world that we are not alone. While many are waiting for a type of disclosure event in which other-worldly beings present themselves and their spacecraft to humanity, we might be surprised to find these beings presenting themselves in a different way. This may begin with an established communication via gravitons.

In September of 2015, for the first time ever, gravitational waves were detected.[36] Before that time, gravity waves, gravitons, and the gravitational quantum field have been largely speculative and theoretical. Gravitons had never been directly observed. The effects of the gravitational field are seen every day, of course (when you drop a ball, it falls), but without actually observing the waves/particles of gravity itself, there is a limit to what can be learned and accomplished. Now

[35] "Brian Greene: Elegant Universe- Nova." YouTube. Accessed February 19, 2025. https://www.youtube.com/watch?v=5XBnH5J-RdU&list=PL8FrJ11-5R8X-iGZ6R6TAe3YjstwG4o7M&index=6.

[36] "Gravitational Waves Detected 100 Years after Einstein's Prediction." Caltech. Accessed February 19, 2025. https://www.ligo.caltech.edu/news/ligo20160211.

that waves of gravity have actually been detected, there's no telling what the ramifications will be.

The detection was achieved by the Laser Interferometer Gravitational-Wave Observatory (LIGO).[37] The actual waves were created by the merging of two black holes: one the mass of twenty-nine suns and the other the mass of thirty-six suns. Each black hole is estimated as being roughly thirty miles in diameter. Gravity waves are so incredibly weak that it takes an extremely sensitive detector like LIGO to be able to detect them. LIGO can measure distortions as small as one-thousandth the size of a proton. The gravity waves LIGO detected lasted only one-fifth of a second. Even more amazing, the detection happened at greater than a five-sigma standard of proof.

On one hand, this discovery is incredibly exciting. After all, an aspect of God's creation has been detected. Another piece of His grand design can now be understood a bit better. However, this could turn to be troubling news if/when mankind decides to use this knowledge for dangerous and potentially disastrous goals.

---

[37] Ibid.

What will this discovery bring? David Reitze, executive director of LIGO, has said, "What's really exciting is what comes next, I think we're opening a window on the universe—a window of gravitational wave astronomy."[38] Kip Thorne, Caltech's Richard P. Feynman Professor of Theoretical Physics, emeritus, is also quoted as saying something nearly identical: that this discovery is opening a new window on the universe.[39] Gravitational wave astronomy and new branches of quantum physics are interesting windows, of course, but what of some other windows that might be opened?

This brings us back to the goal of certain physicists to develop a gravitational communication system. There are steps toward that goal that must be taken, of course. First would be the confirmed discovery of gravitational waves and/ or gravitons themselves. Next would be learning to repeat the detection in a lab by creating gravitons or gravity waves. They would do this by putting Einstein's general theory to the test directly and experimentally. Once that is accomplished, there

[38] "Was It All Just Noise? Independent Analysis Casts Doubt on LIGO's Detections." Big Think, October 17, 2022. https://bigthink.com/starts-with-a-bang/was-it-all-just-noise-independent-analysis-casts-doubt-on-ligos-detections/.

[39] "Nobel Prize in Physics 2017." NobelPrize.org. Accessed February 19, 2025. https://www.nobelprize.org/prizes/physics/2017/thorne/interview/.

will be enough information to go on to learn how to manipulate the gravitons themselves.[40]

Interestingly enough, this detection of gravitational waves occurred in September of 2015, but wasn't officially announced until six months later on February 11, 2016.[41] This leads us to wonder what else has been accomplished and not yet announced. Could these discoveries spur on the opening of the abyss in Revelation chapter 9? Only time will tell, but by the looks of it, we are not too far off from knowing for sure.

This leads us to wonder what the world might look like after interdimensional communication is established. We may have the answer in the prophetic book of Revelation. From the prophet John, Revelation 9:1–3 states:

And the fifth angel sounded, and I saw a star fall from heaven unto the earth: and to him was given the key of the bottomless pit. And he opened the bottomless pit; and there

---

40 40 "Brian Greene: Elegant Universe- Nova." YouTube. Accessed February 19, 2025. https://www.youtube.com/watch?v=5XBnH5J-RdU&list=PL8FrJ11-5R8X-iGZ6R6TAe3YjstwG4o7M&index=6.

41 41 "Gravitational Waves Detected 100 Years after Einstein's Prediction." Caltech. Accessed February 19, 2025. https://www.ligo.caltech.edu/news/ligo20160211.

arose a smoke out of the pit, as the smoke of a great furnace; and the sun and the air were darkened by reason of the smoke of the pit. And there came out of the smoke locusts upon the earth: and unto them was given power, as the scorpions of the earth have power.

The first thing to notice is that this occurs when the fifth angel sounds. In my book Cherubim Chariots, I explore the possibility of the number of cherubim faces in Ezekiel's vision representing spatial dimensions.[42] If we include time, it is correct to say that we are four-dimensional beings (three dimensions of space and one of time). If we follow that logic, we might have a reference to a being of an extra dimension in the fifth trumpet of Revelation (four of space and one of time, equaling five). I also write in Cherubim Chariots about the theory that when the rebellious angels fell from heaven, they may have fallen to what we would call the fourth spatial dimension.

The angel sounding the trumpet is likely not a fallen angel, but instead might be signaling that a fallen being is about to come into the picture. The rest of the first verse of Revelation

---

[42] [42] Available at ProphecyWatchers.com

9 states, "and I saw a star fall from heaven unto the earth: and to him was given the key of the bottomless pit."

This is no ordinary star. According to our modern vernacular, any star that would fall on the earth would utterly destroy it. There does seem to be a connection between stars and angels and, at times, the word "star" can actually represent an angel. We see this alluded to in Revelation 1:20, which states:

The mystery of the seven stars which thou sawest in my right hand, and the seven golden candlesticks. The seven stars are the angels of the seven churches: and the seven candlesticks which thou sawest are the seven churches.

We can also see the star is a being of some sort, because of the words, "unto him was given the key." This star being referred to with the pronoun "him" shows that this is a person of some sort. This could be a person, or being, of four spatial dimensions rather than three. This is most likely referring to a fallen angel.

Verse 2 tells us that the angel opened the bottomless pit with the key. The word "key" comes from the Greek word kleis and can be used as a metaphor for authority. In a sense, this fallen angel was given permission to open the bottomless pit. We also learn in Revelation 1:18 that Jesus Christ Himself held the keys of death and hell, so most likely it was Jesus who granted this authority.

We may ask why Jesus would give permission for a fallen angel to open the bottomless pit. We find the answer in chapter 2, verses 2–11 in the book of Joel:

A day of darkness and of gloominess, a day of clouds and of thick darkness, as the morning spread upon the mountains: a great people and a strong; there hath not been ever the like, neither shall be any more after it, even to the years of many generations. A fire devoureth before them; and behind them a flame burneth: the land is as the garden of Eden before them, and behind them a desolate wilderness; yea, and nothing shall escape them. The appearance of them is as the appearance of horses; and as horsemen, so shall they run. Like the noise of chariots on the tops of mountains shall they leap, like the noise of a flame of fire that devoureth the stubble, as a strong people set in battle array. Before their face the people shall be much pained: all faces shall gather blackness. They shall run like mighty men; they shall climb the wall like men of war; and they shall march every one on his ways, and they shall not break their ranks: Neither shall one thrust another; they shall walk every one in his path: and when they fall upon the sword, they shall not be wounded. They shall run to and fro in the city; they shall run upon the wall, they shall climb up upon the houses; they shall enter in at the windows like a thief. The earth shall quake before them; the heavens shall tremble: the sun and the moon shall be dark, and the stars shall withdraw their shining: And the Lord shall utter his voice before his army: for his camp is very great: for he is strong that executeth his word: for the day of the Lord is great and very terrible; and who can abide it?

We can learn many truths in this passage, but for our purposes here, we only need to note a couple of things. First, notice this army is described in many of the same ways as the locust army of Revelation 9 (and is probably the very same, though there is debate on that point). We also read in verse 8 of their immortality ("when they fall upon the sword, they shall not be wounded"), showing these are likely angelic in nature.

Given the description of the circumstances surrounding these beings (sun, moon, and stars darkened, clouds of thick darkness, etc.), they seem to be the very same locust-beings from Revelation 9. But also notice that Joel 2:11 says this is the Lord's army. How can this be?

First, and quite simply, this could be a different group altogether from the locust army. This could be the army of obedient angels that gather mankind to judgment at the return of Christ. This would make sense because in the Joel passage, it says "A fire devoureth before them; and behind them a flame burneth: the land is as the garden of Eden before them, and behind them a desolate wilderness; yea, and nothing shall escape them." This seems to indicate that the land itself will be destroyed, but in Revelation it says the locusts cannot hurt any green thing. Therefore, it could be as simple as this is an entirely different army altogether. But what if it's not; is it possible that God could use the locust army to accomplish His goals?

There are times in the Bible when God will use the enemy for His own purposes. After all, He is ultimately in control of these things anyway; He can use them as He sees fit. For example, in the book of Exodus, we read that God hardened Pharaoh's heart (Exodus 9:12). We also read later in Revelation chapter 9:

And the sixth angel sounded, and I heard a voice from the four horns of the golden altar which is before God, Saying to the sixth angel which had the trumpet, Loose the four angels which are bound in the great river Euphrates. And the four angels were loosed, which were prepared for an hour, and a day, and a month, and a year, for to slay the third part of men.

As we can see, there are times the Lord will use the enemy to fulfill His own purposes, usually in the way of judgment. The locust army, if it is the same as the Joel army, is no different.

Going back to the differences between the Joel and Revelation armies, there might be other ways to reconcile these two seemingly different descriptions. An easy way would be to point out that the Joel passage doesn't say that the devouring fire is actually caused by the locusts themselves, that could be a secondary thing. It also could be that the "land" and "desolate wilderness" could be a way of just describing provisions and supplies. It could be a way of saying "they had everything they wanted before the locusts came, and when they were done, they had nothing," seemingly because they are in so much pain for 5 months that the only thing they're concerned with is their own deaths, but they can't even make that happen, so their provisions, wealth, and other things are pointless at that time.

However it all plays out, before the Revelation locust army is unleashed into our world, the gravitational communication aspect becomes more obvious as we consider these prophecies. It is possible that the LHC at CERN will detect evidence of gravitons which, in turn, could lead to a communication device to higher-dimensional entities. After all, what particle but the graviton could best represent fallen angels? We even have reference to falling, an effect caused by gravity, in the description of the star/angel that opens the bottomless pit.

Abaddon and the Ezekiel Antithesis

It is entirely possible that these locusts are the direct antithesis of the cherubim Ezekiel saw in chapter 1 of his book. For everything God has, Satan has an evil and inferior duplicate. Satan has never had an original thought of his own, so he borrows from God. When we look closely at the description of these locusts and compare it to Ezekiel's vision, we see they are complete opposites. The locust army is very likely comprised of fallen cherubim. They are most likely described as locusts because of the destructive role they play, not necessarily because of their physical appearance, which is described in Revelation 9:7 as "and the shapes of the locusts were like unto horses prepared unto battle."

As shown in Cherubim Chariots, the cherubim seem to be an amalgamation of human and animal appearances. Other ancient cultures seem to have witnessed these things as well, such as the Lamassu and Shedu of ancient Assyria. These beings were described as having an animal body, such as a bull or a lion, with wings and a human head. In Ezekiel's vision of the cherubim, we see an opposite description: Ezekiel describes animal heads atop human-like, winged bodies. We also see in Ezekiel's vision that one of the faces is described as being half human, half lion, and bisected vertically. However, Revelation 9:7–8 states:

And the shapes of the locusts were like unto horses prepared unto battle; and on their heads were as it were crowns like gold, and their faces were as the faces of men. And they had hair as the hair of women, and their teeth were as the teeth of lions.

If they had faces of men, yet teeth of lions, it would suggest a half-human, half-lion face, but bisected horizontally rather than vertically. This could be another attribute to show these locusts are the antithesis of the heavenly cherubim Ezekiel witnessed.

Ezekiel described the heavenly cherubim as carrying the throne of God on top of them. Revelation 9:11 states:

And they had a king over them, which is the angel of the bottomless pit, whose name in the Hebrew tongue is Abaddon, but in the Greek tongue hath his name Apollyon.

The word "over" comes from the Greek word *epi*, which can mean "upon" as well as represent a statement of authority. There are times the Bible uses the word *epi* to describe something physically on top of something else without regard to authoritative position. Much how the heavenly cherubim were carrying the true God over them, these fallen cherubim seem to be carrying their false god and king, Abaddon.

As pointed out in Cherubim Chariots, the ancient world likely had direct contact with fallen cherubim, though they called them things like Lamassu and Shedu. It is possible that the book of Revelation is prophesying a return of these fallen creatures. It's also possible, if interdimensional contact is made through the use of gravitons, it will be either these fallen cherubim or the king over them that humanity will be in contact with.

As shown earlier, the area where CERN is located today is thought to have been dedicated to this same false god in ancient times. Perhaps that dedication will manifest itself in the near future. The idea behind all of this is that it is possible the mechanism of opening the abyss, at least on the human, physical side, is to open a communication system with gravitons or to breach the barrier between dimensions in order to explore what's there, and while that's happening on the physical side, on the spiritual side God is allowing humans to do this and an angel is permitted to open the bottomless pit, thereby releasing these horrific fallen cherubim on the world.

It's like God saying "alright, you want to contact extra dimensional entities that I clearly separated from you for your protection, you don't want my protection, then fine, you'll get exactly what you want, here's the false gods you keep going after, let's see how they treat you." At that point, hell is literally poured out on the earth.

Now, of course, the bottomless pit and release of the locusts prophecy in Revelation 9 might not have anything to do with CERN, so I don't want to create this spirit of fear around it. Even if we as believers were here during this prophecy, and I don't believe we will be, but even if we were, the prophecy says this is only going to affect nonbelievers, these things are not allowed to hurt followers of God, only those who reject Him, so for us as Christians, there is nothing for us to worry about. These things are the false gods people have always rejected God for, and these people are getting exactly what they want, they are getting to commune with their gods, that's their punishment. If you belong to Jesus, this punishment is not for you.

Even more, you'll get to commune with your God as well, but instead of it being a horrific, abusive experience, it'll be wonderful, beautiful, and exactly what you were created for. So, if you don't know Jesus today, you should get to know him right now, start a relationship with Him, change your mind about Him, believe in Him, pray and ask to take part in His promised salvation after this life passes; one thing is for sure, you will die some day. You don't want to run the risk of running into horrible beings like this. You want to make sure you're protected and that your entrance into God's eternal Kingdom is secure. Today's the day to get that taken care of, right now, call out to Jesus and be spiritually born again in His name.

Chapter 15: Deceptions of Edgar Cayce

Now that we have the background about our true, spiritual enemy, we can look at what demonic doctrines are going around the world today. What is our enemy teaching the unbelieving (and sometimes eve the believing) world and how can we defend against it? This is an important question because there are many false doctrines plaguing the world right now.

For those who aren't familiar with me and my testimony, I was brought up in a Christian home but, in my early adulthood, fell into New Age theology for a few years. It began because I was dealing with sleep paralysis. I was also experiencing, what I considered to be, demonic manifestations and attacks. I didn't know anything about spiritual warfare and had no idea how to solve this problem. I confided in a friend about my problem and she handed me a book about astral projection. Before that time, I had never heard of such a thing. Her idea was I could use astral projection (the process of meditating in order to leave your own physical body) to escape the attacks. I felt it was worth a shot.

I practiced and meditated, even becoming a vegetarian (something the book suggested), for six months before it actually happened. This was when I discovered that, yes, astral projection is fully real and not just a dream, hallucination, or product of imagination. Once I became better at it, I decided to test it. I would astral project into places I've never been before, then later visit those places to see if the projections were accurate. They were. Every time.

I quickly found out there would be no way astral projection could help me with my sleep paralysis and demonic attack problem. The type of meditation needed would have been impossible under such strenuous conditions. In fact, there were times when meditation would spur on sleep paralysis and subsequent demonic manifestations. Regardless, I was already hooked. I didn't care. For me at the time, it was well worth it.

By this time, I was becoming more and more entrenched in New Age theology. One of my favorite people to read about was Edgar Cayce. Stories of him falling asleep on a Bible as a child and waking up with full recall of scripture absolutely fascinated me. Even the depiction of his self-sacrifice; continuing to use his gifts for the benefit of others until it eventually killed him, really spoke to me. At the time, I was thinking, now here is a good man and an example of what the world needs more of. It was easy for me to justify Cayce's New Age theology by believing he was truly a Christian and everything else he taught was just an extension of that. Of course, this was during a time when I wasn't taking the Bible very seriously and was going out of my way to ignore all of the inconsistencies between Edgar Cayce and the Bible.

A couple of years after my first introduction to Edgar Cayce, I renounced everything New Age. The short version of the story is, while astral projecting, I came across a group of spiritual beings who, at the time, seemed very friendly. They told me they would help me leave my body if I asked them to. The next time I tried to astral project, I couldn't. However, I decided not to ask the entities for help. Shortly after that, our home came under a spiritual attack that I did not think was possible outside of horror movies. Basically, the entities were upset that I didn't invite them in, so to speak, so they were trying to force their way in. This put me on a path to getting back into the Bible, rededicating my life to Christ, learning about spiritual warfare, and using the authority in the name of Jesus to force these things out. It worked. Not only did it solve that problem, but it also ended up completely solving my issue with sleep paralysis and demonic manifestations. Because of Jesus Christ, I no longer have to live in fear of those things.

This new spiritual transformation caused me to look at New Age theology through a truthful lens. Suddenly I felt awake and could not believe the types of things I was involved in. Looking at Edgar Cayce through a biblical lens was especially eye-opening. Once I realized what a Christian actually is, any belief I had that Edgar Cayce was a true follower of Christ was dispelled.

Now, to be clear, I am not saying Edgar Cayce wasn't saved. Besides God, no one can know that. For all anyone knows, Cayce could have repented at the end of his life. No one knows. However, being saved and being a follower of

Christ are a bit different. Accepting Jesus as your savior is the first initial step toward a relationship with God. Actively cultivating that relationship, however, is what it means to be a follower of Christ.

Edgar Cayce might have accepted Jesus at some point. He might be in Heaven right now. We have no way of knowing. However, if he never repented and left this world apart from Christ, then all hope for him is lost. While we might not know exactly where he ended up in eternity, we do have the information available to deduce, based on biblical premises, if he was a true follower of Christ or not. One of the biggest evidences we can look at are his prophecies.

In Jesus' own words, Matthew 7:15-20 reads:

15 Beware of false prophets, which come to you in sheep's clothing, but inwardly they are ravening wolves. 16 Ye shall know them by their fruits. Do men gather grapes of thorns, or figs of thistles? 17 Even so every good tree bringeth forth good fruit; but a corrupt tree bringeth forth evil fruit. 18 A good tree cannot bring forth evil fruit, neither can a corrupt tree bring forth good fruit. 19 Every tree that bringeth not forth good fruit is hewn down, and cast into the fire. 20 Wherefore by their fruits ye shall know them.

Jesus tells us we can know someone, specifically false prophets, by their fruits. What have they produced? What was the cause or motivation of their actions? Did they win people to the Lord or lead them astray?

Edgar Cayce is not known for bringing people to salvation through Jesus Christ. In fact, Cayce is most known for his large number of prophecies. Specific numbers vary on just how many prophecies and other writings there are of Cayce's, but they are usually counted as somewhere around 20,000. He also had a vast array of teachings, including things about astral travel, the Akashic records, and reincarnation. Here is one source of interpretation of Cayce's teachings:

Cayce predicted that the so-called "Battle of Armageddon" described symbolically in the Bible would begin in 1999. Cayce foresaw that this "battle" will not be a war fought on Earth. Rather, it will be a spiritual struggle between the "higher forces of light" and "lower forces of darkness" for 1000 years of Earth time. The reason for this struggle is to prevent souls from lower afterlife realms from reincarnating to Earth. By preventing souls from the lower afterlife realms from reincarnating to Earth, only enlightened souls will be permitted to reincarnate. The result will be 1000 years of building a world of peace and enlightenment. After 1000 years, souls from lower afterlife realms will be permitted once again to reincarnate to Earth. By this time, the so-called "kingdom of heaven" will have been established on Earth.[43]

This type of teaching is common in New Age theology; I remember it quite well. However, we can see how New Age theology and Edgar Cayce's teachings are incompatible with the Bible. In this example, the first thing to point out is the battle of Armageddon did not begin in 1999. Also, there is nothing in the scriptures to signify this is meant to be understood as symbolic. The specific text, Revelation 16:16-21, reads:

16 And he gathered them together into a place called in the Hebrew tongue Armageddon. 17 And the seventh angel poured out his vial into the air; and there came a great voice out of the temple of heaven, from the throne, saying, It is done. 18 And there were voices, and thunders, and lightnings;

---

[43] "Home." Predictions for 2023 Alamongordo Prophecies for the future. Accessed February 24, 2025. http://www.alamongordo.com/the-edgar-cayce-predictions/.

and there was a great earthquake, such as was not since men were upon the earth, so mighty an earthquake, and so great. 19 And the great city was divided into three parts, and the cities of the nations fell: and great Babylon came in remembrance before God, to give unto her the cup of the wine of the fierceness of his wrath. 20 And every island fled away, and the mountains were not found. 21 And there fell upon men a great hail out of heaven, every stone about the weight of a talent: and men blasphemed God because of the plague of the hail; for the plague thereof was exceeding great.

We have very literal language used here. There is talk of angels, of course, but this is not an event that is happening in Heaven or another spiritual location. We read about an earthly place called "Armageddon" in the Hebrew language, a physical earthquake, an earthly city, earthly islands, earthly mountains, earthly men, and hail falling on the earth. These are all physical and literal things mentioned throughout the text. Therefore, if Cayce taught the battle would not be on Earth, we have a choice to make. Are we going to believe Edgar Cayce or the Bible? Either the Bible contains the truth or not. Biblical teachings compared against Edgar Cayce's teachings offer no middle ground nor compromise.

Reincarnation is a big belief taught by Cayce and other more modern New Age sources. However, Hebrews 9:27 states:

And as it is appointed unto men once to die, but after this the judgment:

Again, we have a choice. Are we going to believe Cayce or the Bible? The Bible teaches once you die, you are sealed in your eternal choice. Either you have accepted Jesus or rejected Him. You have either followed God or you haven't. Cayce taught reincarnation. These two beliefs cannot go hand in hand without compromising one or the other.

Then the question inevitably comes up, did Edgar Cayce have prophesies that turned out true? Yes. In fact, he is regarded as one of the greatest worldly prophets because, based on certain estimations, he has over an 80% accuracy rating. Does this mean he was a Christian? Quite simply, no.

The Bible teaches that anything less than a 100% accuracy rating in the realm of prophecy is unacceptable. In fact, in the ancient days of Israel, one false prophecy was enough to earn a death sentence. This is because any prophecy of God will come to pass exactly as it was prophesied. However, a prophecy by any other source will never be able to have that kind of accuracy. This is how we can tell if a prophet is representing God or not. YHWH, the God of the Bible, takes prophecy very seriously. Jesus consistently warned against false prophets, and the Old Testament give us the method to tell if a prophet is true or false. Deuteronomy 18:19-22 reads:

19 And it shall come to pass, that whosoever will not hearken unto my words which he shall speak in my name, I will require it of him. 20 But the prophet, which shall presume to speak a word in my name, which I have not commanded him to speak, or that shall speak in the name of other gods, even that prophet shall die. 21 And if thou say in thine heart, How shall we know the word which the Lord hath not spoken? 22 When a prophet speaketh in the name of the Lord, if the thing follow not, nor come to pass, that is the thing which the Lord hath not spoken, but the prophet hath spoken it presumptuously: thou shalt not be afraid of him.

Therefore, we once again have a contradiction between the Bible and Edgar Cayce. Which do we trust? The Bible holds up to its own teachings by providing a 100% prophetic accuracy rating. The Bible has been help up to scrutiny for millennia, yet has never been disproved. The great thing about all this is it should be incredibly easy to disprove the Bible if it weren't true. All one would have to do is find one prophecy that didn't come to pass when and how God said it would. Many have tried and all have failed.

I don't say these things to be insensitive or rude. I completely understand the allure of the New Age. However, once I was out of it and started seeing things clearly, I realized the reality behind all the things I was inherently interested in was found in the Bible. Personally, I absolutely love prophecy. I love the idea that I have a book at my disposal that consistently tells the future before it happens. Of course, the world will claim this isn't true, but also offers no real evidence to back up that claim. Again, if the Bible were not true, it should be incredibly easy to disprove.

As I stated before, the purpose here is not to insult Edgar Cayce or show disrespect to any person. I don't hate or hold anything against Cayce personally. My belief is he was more of a victim; a deceived person who believed was doing good and right by the world, but who the forces of darkness were using towards their own ends. I see people like Edgar Cayce as prisoners or war rather than the enemy. The truth, the biblical truth, is that our true enemy is not each other. In essence, people aren't the problem. As we saw earlier, Ephesians 6:12 teaches us the true enemy is a spiritual one. It reads:

For we wrestle not against flesh and blood, but against principalities, against powers, against the rulers of the darkness of this world, against spiritual wickedness in high places.

Fallen angels and demons are our true enemy. They are the ones who are sowing discord amongst humanity. They are the true promulgators of deception. However, that doesn't let us off the hook either. We all have a personal responsibility to find the truth and share it with others through God's lead. That is my hope here.

My main reason for writing this is the hope that there might be people who are beginning to question New Age and want more information. This isn't an attempt to prove myself right or slam people who subscribe to New Age beliefs. If you are into New Age theology, I don't hate you, I don't blame you, and I don't judge you. I would be the biggest hypocrite in the world if I did. Instead, my only concern is to provide you with the evidence of truth and hope you will consider it seriously and logically.

Chapter 16: Prayer in the Labyrinth

If there was ever a time Christianity could use Mark Flynn's groundbreaking book Forbidden Secrets of the Labyrinth, it is now. In his book, Flynn explains the importance of the labyrinth in ancient times as well as what it means for us today.[44] The enemy has humanity entranced in the labyrinth, and now the Church is embracing it.

The labyrinth, in various forms, can be found all throughout ancient pagan religions. Mosaics of labyrinths can even be found on the floors of Freemason lodges. Now, Christianity has joined the trend.

---

[44] Flynn, Mark A. Forbidden secrets of the labyrinth: The awakened ones, the hidden destiny of America, and the Day After Tomorrow. Crane, Mo: Defender, 2014.

In an article entitled "Labyrinth transforms prayer life, Baptists say", Baptist News Global reported on a growing trend in the Baptist church. The article states:

The ancient practice which involves walking a maze while praying has become more popular among Baptists as Christians in general are adopting more eclectic spiritual disciplines.[45]

Rita Martin, one who practices this ritual, is described in the article as well:

Martin said she has "always been a pray-er" but now sees her mind often drifted off during normal prayer times.

The labyrinth "is a very good tool to keep your mind on track and to concentrate on what you're praying for, and why you're praying and just communing with God."

Martin said her Baptist upbringing offered no opposition to the practice, especially after she realized the leavening effect it's had on her spiritual life overall.

---

[45] Brumley, Jeff. "Labyrinth Transforms Prayer Life, Baptists Say." Baptist News Global, May 7, 2014. https://baptistnews.com/article/labyrinth-transforms-prayer-life-baptists-say/.

"I'm thinking, why have we never done this before?"

Her Baptist upbringing offered no position on this practice and she is left wondering why they had not done it before. Despite the apparent spiritual benefits of the practice (which, of course, is never stated in the Bible for us to take part in), Mark Flynn explains in his book why the labyrinth is a tool of the enemy. Yet, Christianity as a whole sees no problem with this practice.

Another article describes the restoration of the prayer labyrinth at a different Baptist church.[46] It states:

A group of church members spent the past two months restoring the labyrinth and hopes it again serves as a peaceful reflection spot for residents throughout Waco. It is open to the public and will be formally rededicated in April.

"It needs to be used," church member Marie Allen said. "It's a beautiful space and it's meaningful."

---

[46] Prayer Labyrinth restored near Lake Shore Baptist Church. Accessed February 24, 2025. https://wacotrib.com/news/local/prayer-labyrinth-restored-near-lake-shore-baptist-church/article_bc6d8ab6-98b6-53d2-8f0b-24cd8284dd2e.html.

Unlike mazes, a labyrinth has one path and a single entry/ exit point. Walkers follow the path around until it meets a dead-end center point, the turnaround and return to the starting point, using the journey for personal reflection or prayer.

"I've seen people reach that center point and just start sobbing," said Sandy Londos, another church member who worked on the labyrinth. "Other times, I've seen people get to the center and just (exhale)."

The labyrinth was the brainchild of Lake Shore Baptist member Becky Henderson, who designed the path and insisted that it be wide enough to accommodate people in wheelchairs. The church finished it in 2003 after Henderson died unexpectedly, naming it in her honor.

Rick Allen, who is not related to Marie Allen, said in addition to couples and children walking the labyrinth, some therapists asked to use it to help their clients open up more during sessions.

He personally used it in teaching lessons on prayer to teen members in a Wednesday night Bible study course in the spring.

"When I would go through the labyrinth, I would say to myself, 'Stay on the path, stay on the path,' and that became not only a mantra but also a metaphor for things that were going on in my life," he said.

Vain repetitions (mantras) and opening occult practices up to children; what will be next for Christianity?

The irony in all of this is what the labyrinth truly represents according to Mark Flynn. Greek mythology states the labyrinth was set up with a Minotaur in the center. The story tells us King Minos (who has been associated with the Canaanite deity Baal Meon) prayed to Poseidon for help to become the most powerful king. Poseidon then sent him the "Cretan Bull", which was perfect and snow-white. Minos kept the bull rather than sacrificing it to Poseidon and instead sacrificed a substitute bull. As a punishment, Poseidon had Aphrodite cause the wife of Minos, Pasiphae, to fall in love with the white bull. Pasiphae then committed adulterous acts with the white bull (which was actually Zeus in disguise), and the result was a terrifying half-bull, half-man abomination. This was the Minotaur. The Minotaur required human flesh and was too difficult to control, so Minos, by direction of the Delphi Oracle, commissioned Daedalus to create a huge labyrinth to imprison the monster. From time to time, humans were sent in to the labyrinth as a type of sacrifice to the Minotaur. Later, Theseus (the demigod son of Aegeus and Poseidon) managed to enter the labyrinth and kill the Minotaur.

According to Flynn, this story if rife with symbolism that shows the plan of the enemy. When assigning identities to mythological characters, it is important to remember these stories are being told from the perspective of the enemy, meaning roles are reversed. From the enemy's perspective, the labyrinth represents the lives we lead in the physical world, the Minotaur represents Christ, and Theseus represents the antichrist. With these representations, the whole antichrist plan of the enemy is explained for us in the story of the labyrinth.

It is the plan of the enemy to usurp the things of, and effectively kill, God Himself, thereby freeing the inhabitants of the world from the labyrinth God has put in place. With churches taking on the occultic and mystical practice of walking the labyrinth in prayer, it is clear the enemy is plunging the church into deception. Of course, this isn't the first time this has happened. There has also been the introduction of yoga, angel prayer, and human worship into the Christian church.

If we don't do our due diligence to learn about these things, we will find ourselves falling into deception. We need to stay informed so we do not inadvertently become tricked into worshiping the serpent. As we looked at before, Hosea 4:6 states:

My people are destroyed for lack of knowledge: because thou hast rejected knowledge, I will also reject thee, that thou shalt be no priest to me: seeing thou hast forgotten the law of thy God, I will also forget thy children.

Chapter 17: New Age Beliefs in the Church

As I've stated before, I fully believe we are living in the end times just before the tribulation is set to occur. When we look at prophecies surrounding the tribulation, we know there will be a one-world religion. Many have speculated on what that could be.

Some have argued that it will be a type of new age religion that will teach man is his own god and the individual is above all else with the false prophet and antichrist as type of spirit guides. The groundwork for this end-times religion is already in place and, most concerning, it's even taken root in the Church.

Introduction

As I stated earlier, years ago, I was involved in new age theology; heavily. I was always the type of person that liked to look at alternate explanations of things, and new age theology pandered to that perfectly for me. I bought into the hype. The strange thing was, at the time I was involved in these things, I was calling myself a Christian. I never would have identified myself as a "new ager" or "gnostic" or any of the other names sometimes attributed to the many, many paths of new age theology. At the time, I thought I knew the Bible pretty well. After all, I was born and raised in a Baptist environment. This, in my mind, granted me the permission to claim I pretty much knew the basics of everything in the Bible (even the parts I had not personally read).

When I became interested in new age theology, I thought I had found the other end of Christianity: the completion of the Bible. I thought I had found answers that the Bible didn't provide. Little did I know, though I should have, the Bible provided every answer I was looking for at the time. I would have known that had I bothered to open it up myself. Instead, I found myself believing astral projection and remote viewing were good and beneficial practices; a way for my consciousness to enter heavenly realms whenever I wanted. I believed people like Edgar Cayce were literal prophets of God, even though they never preached repentance, salvation only through Jesus Christ, or 100% accurate prophecy. I was believing I was talking with angels and spirit guides, even though they played to my ego by being way more interested in me than the Lord Jesus Christ, His divinity, and His gift of eternal salvation.

Eventually, God showed me the deception of new age. Once the enemy was exposed, they didn't come across as nice angels or caring spirit guides anymore. No, they were hideous demonic entities only interested in destroying me and my family. The truth was out. It was only the power and authority in the name of Jesus Christ, the true Son of God, that banished these entities and closed all the spiritual doors I had inadvertently opened by way of my previous new age practices.

This was when God led me to a community of Christians who knew how to read the Bible, preach truth, expose lies, discern reality, and teach the true gospel of Jesus Christ. Through God, the Bible, and this community, I was (and still am) able to find all the answers I was looking for when I first got into new age theology. I began seeing real manifestations of truth, instead of the deceptions the enemy was providing earlier. I rededicated my life to Christ (which I consider to be my true salvation experience) and began working with what God gave me. I started to research and study as much as possible, then began writing my own books and producing a podcast.

I have been doing this for over ten years now. One thing I realize is much of the Church is still ignorant to what new age theology teaches. This isn't a criticism exactly; after all, new age theology is spiritually damaging and should be avoided at all costs. The problem is, however, sometimes new age theology is packaged as Christian doctrine and Christians may or may not always know the difference. Because of this, sometimes new age teachings are introduced to believers unknowingly and, unfortunately, these teachings spread like a cancer; or perhaps more accurately, like leaven in bread. Therefore, my purpose here is to provide you, the audience, with a few of the teachings and buzz words so you can know what to stay away from.

This is not exhaustive; there is much, much more out there than what is just presented here. However, it is my hope this will provoke you, if you hear any of these things being taught, to research things out before believing them at face value. Also, I would ask that if you do hear someone claiming to be a Christian and preaching these things, pray for that person in all love and humility. A person like that would be under heavy spiritual attack and deception. Instead of viewing that type of person as an enemy, think of them as a prisoner of war who needs our help. Remember, we wrestle not against flesh and blood. Of course, that does not mean we tolerate the bad teaching. If someone teaches this stuff, you should back away from them at all costs, but pray for them from afar nonetheless.

The 13th Dimension and Anti-Semitism

One thing about new age theology is there isn't a previously established and accepted "truth" that everything else is measured against. There is no "new age bible" that every new ager believes in whole-heartedly. New age is a theology that accepts basically anything and everything, so long as it's not Christianity, of course. But Buddhism, Zoroastrianism, Gnosticism, Hinduism, and any number of others fit in perfectly to new age. Because of this, it is hard to say "all new agers believe" or even "new age teaches"

135

because some factions may while others may not. New age really differs slightly from individual to individual. It is an all-you-can-eat belief; everything is included. This is part of what makes it so deceptive. It is easy to include elements of Christianity and the Bible into new age teaching, then call the whole thing Christian.

One teaching within new age theology is that of the 13th dimension. Usually, when new agers talk about "dimensions", they do not mean the physical or temporal dimensions quantum physics talk about (though, at times, this is incorporated). They are usually speaking of stages of spiritual ascension. For example, consider this excerpt from "A NEW ORDER OF THE AGES: A Metaphysical Blueprint of Reality and an Exposé on Powerful Reptilian/Aryan Bloodlines (Vol. 2)" (Aug 1, 2011) by Collin Robert Bowling. On page 319:

"The Universal Consciousness (Prime Creator) projects itself from the 13th dimension (infinite possibilities, the Void) down a straight line through the 5th dimension (pure love) and splays it out in a four-dimensional creation we all call the physical manifest world. We are all simply tiny aspects of the

Universal Consciousness projecting ourselves into the world and interacting with it."[47]

The idea here is that there is a piece of their god in all of us. This stems from Gnosticism, which teaches there is a piece of the Light in all of us (which transcends even YHWH, who in Gnosticism is an ignorant being who was created essentially by mistake) and when we come to that realization, we are eternally saved. This is a clear deception and heresy.

In that same book, there is also a number of anti-Semetic teachings. Here is one:

"The Jewish people seem to have had a hard time throughout history, and you might now be wondering who the Jews really are. The globalist Zionists (the Learned Elders of Zion), the House of David and the members of the Druidic Council are not Jews. They have commandeered that race creed and use it as a front for power and greed. Think all Jewish people are greedy and they hoard power? No, the Zionists and Druids are greedy and they hoard power...The truth is that the overwhelmingly majority of Jewish people, and

---

[47] Bowling, Collin Robert. A new order of the ages: A metaphysical blueprint of Reality and an exposé on powerful reptilian. Bloomington Indiana: iUniverse, Inc, 2011.

certainly those that control Israel, have no historical connection to this area, are not genetically Jewish and are not Semites. The globalists who control Israel are working for the House of David and the Illuminati."

Again, this just shows the level of depravity and deception that can run rampant in some of these circles.

The anti-Semitism speaks to the level of deception promoted in books such as these and the extreme level of spiritual discernment needed in navigating them. Satan has always been about the destruction of the Jewish people and anti-Semitism. It is my belief one of the more recent tactics to discredit the people of Israel is this idea that "the Jews in Israel aren't the real Jews." Unfortunately, this is something that has been promulgated throughout the Church as well.

Chakras, Light, and Universal Connectivity

Sometimes connected with the idea of dimensions is the teaching of Chakras. In most new age belief systems, Chakras are taught as types of energy power centers that run up your spine. Usually it is taught there are seven of these (though sometimes is taught there are fifteen or more). The idea is, during meditation, to concentrate on opening each chakra, from the base of your spine to the crown of your head, each time keeping the previous in mind.

Once you open the seventh and keep the remaining six open, you are supposed to experience inner peace and a type of nirvana-connection to the universe. This is also sometimes taught in yoga classes.

Along with this, it is also sometimes taught that we are beings of light. Again, this is not talking about the light of God of the Bible or even light from the scientific perspective. From the Bible, it is true that God said "Let there be light". Yet, this is not when human beings were created. Scientifically speaking, light is made up of individual and indivisible packets called "photons". Photons are massless and fundamental particles.

Human beings, on a quantum level, are made up of atoms, which include electrons, protons, neutrons, quarks, gluons, and forces. Simply speaking, we are not made of only light; not from a biblical nor a scientific perspective. But, in bringing this up, notice how easy it is for someone to control the conversation if they know the right words to say. "But, God is light, God created light, and God created you, so you are the light and love of God." See how easy it is to make these things sound Christian?

In truth, the Bible makes a clear distinction between God, creation, and humans. We humans are put in charge of the world, to take care of it. God created the world and the universe, but they are still distinctly separate things from God. God is not the universe. He is not the world. We humans are not God. God is God. We are human beings. The world is the world and the universe is the universe. There is a connection in that God created all of it, but nowhere in the Bible are we asked to actively attempt to tap into that connection. We are, however, asked to have a personal relationship with God, in which the only mediator is Jesus Christ. Not the universe. Not the world. Not each other. Just Jesus.

The Third Eye and/or Pineal Gland

The idea of the third eye in connection to the pineal gland of the brain is popular among much new age teaching. Unfortunately, it's growing in popularity among Christians as well. The way it is often presented to Christians is by saying it is the pineal gland that is activated during prayer. Something also sometimes said is that there is a worldwide conspiracy to calcify the pineal gland, usually by fluoridated water, thereby preventing us from being able to pray effectively.

Think of where this leads. This teaching essentially states if you aren't getting your prayers answered or if you feel God is far from you, it is not because of a possible sin in your life or something you need to repent of; it is due to forces outside of your control (and apparently outside of God's control too), so you might as well accept it or find a way around it. The way around it they suggest is usually meditation, opening chakras, doing various cleanses, and opening yourself to the universal connection we all supposedly share. Of course, the biblical solution is much simpler and completely different. Repent and pray without ceasing.

Jesus in the Flesh

This is a big one and, within new age teaching, is usually saved for last because it is a direct attack on a very important tenant of Christian belief. If a person leads with this, chances are they will lose half the audience immediately. However, if a person works to this gradually, they have a higher chance at convincing the majority. There are many ways this is presented, but the basic premise is to deny the flesh aspect of Jesus Christ. Usually people teaching this will say something along the lines of "the pregnancy of Mary was an implantation and not a conception". They will deny that Mary, from a biological level, had any part in the conception of Jesus. Simply speaking, Mary didn't provide the egg. They will say that an already-conceived organism, such as a zygote or a fetus, was implanted into Mary. The problem with this is it completely denies Jesus Christ came in the flesh, because it denies the entire flesh aspect of His conception. 1 John 1-3 states:

1 Beloved, believe not every spirit, but try the spirits whether they are of God: because many false prophets are gone out into the world. 2 Hereby know ye the Spirit of God: Every spirit that confesseth that Jesus Christ is come in the flesh is of God: 3 And every spirit that confesseth not that Jesus Christ is come in the flesh is not of God: and this is that spirit of antichrist, whereof ye have heard that it should come; and even now already is it in the world.

Jesus is God, of course, but if He also wasn't fully human, then He would not be able to represent us for the forgiveness of our sins, rendering His death pointless. Because of this, and because of the clear teachings of the Bible, Jesus was most definitely conceived, not implanted.

As stated earlier, this is far from an exhaustive study into new age influences in the Christian church. However, if this is all new to you, this can be used as a springboard for further study. Most importantly, we should be operating in spiritual discernment. If something someone says doesn't feel quite right, we should look into it and see where these teachings come from. If we hear someone claiming to be a Christian and teaching these types of things, we should expose the heresy, yes, but we should also pray for that person in love and humility. Pray that God will open that person's heart to the truth, see the deception he or she is under, repent, and come back into the fold to be a powerful warrior for Christ rather than Satan.

Remember, as Ephesians 6 teaches us, we wrestle not against flesh and blood. Our enemy is a spiritual one. Let us not fall into the ways of the enemy, based in fear, hatred, and anger. Instead, let us follow God in love, humility, respect, and a humble spirit.

Chapter 18: The Chaos Dragon and New Age

It is popular in the modern world, especially within New Age, to think of God as an impersonal force rather than as a personal Father. This gets fleshed out in a variety of ways as we will shortly see, but how often have we heard people, sometimes even Christians, lament that their prayers are not being answered? Many times, when people feel this way, they see the prayers of their friends being answered, yet not their own. "Why didn't it work for me?" they might be inclined to ask.

In the secular world, this plays out when people notice that others seem to be accomplishing and achieving more in life. They notice good things happening to less-deserving, or even bad, people, and bad things happening to themselves. It is almost as if there is an subconscious belief in the principles fairness, justice, and equality. Yet, these principles are generally believed to be abstract forces at work in the universe somehow, rather than the properties of a divine being.

In New Age, spirit guides, Ascended Masters, and angels are regarded as having personalities, but the overall governing force of the universe is generally seen as lacking personhood. During meditation, the goal is more to tap into a universal energy field at the heart of nature rather than to communicate personally with a transcendent creator. If there is any communication, it is generally with a spirit being lower in the hierarchical rankings than the all-pervading impersonal force of the universe. Ironically, a personal relationship with this force is impossible because it is not a person, meaning it has no awareness, free will, rationality, etc. It cannot reciprocate or interact with you and your intentions. It is like turning on a microwave and trying to have a relationship with the frequencies it emits.

Christianity is different. It offers something richer and deeper than trying to tap into an impersonal force or energy field. The Bible describes a God who is a person, not a force, and who loves His children. Of course, because we are all subject to our modern culture at times, Christians can fall into the trap of inadvertently treating God as a force rather than a person. If God is a force and if a prayer is answered favorably for one person, then that same prayer, if said in the same way, should be answered the same, no matter who utters it. Yet, this is not the case. While New Age (along with Satanism and witchcraft) relies on practices to achieve desired results, Christianity understands God as a person whom the individual must speak with. If there is a desire, the Christian is expected to ask God. At that time, God, through His wisdom, may decide to answer the prayer favorably or unfavorably. In short, prayer is not a spell or incantation. Prayer is speaking with God. If a question is asked, it is up to God how He will answer it.

This is similar to how a good father interacts with his children. At the time of this writing, I have five kids, and while I love them all equally, I interact with them in different ways because they are all unique individuals. Each child has his or her own strengths, weaknesses, and ways of communicating with me.

My youngest child, Anya, is only 4 years old at the time of this writing, so verbal communication with her is limited. However, I show her she is loved in different ways—for example, by playing with her and chasing her through the house. My oldest daughter, Jaklynn, is 14, so she can understand a lot more than Anya or my other daughter, Lilly (who is 6). Lilly is learning things now that Jaklynn has already learned. Also, because each has different interests and ways of looking at the world, communication and interaction are a bit different. For example, Jaklynn communicates more verbally while Anya would rather be doing something to interact with me, such as drawing.

There are situations in which Jaklynn and Lilly could both ask me for the same thing, and I might say yes to one but no to the other. For example, Jaklynn might ask to stay up an hour past her bedtime. Because I've let her do this before and she has proved that she can get up without issue the next morning for school, I might tell her yes. If Lilly were to ask, however, I might say no, because of her age and her attitude when she doesn't get enough sleep. It doesn't mean she did anything wrong. It doesn't mean I love Jaklynn more. It only means they are individuals with their own strengths and weaknesses.

According to Christianity, our relationship with our children can serve as an example of how God interacts with us. We all have a personal relationship with Him. We are all individuals. God Himself is an individual with likes and dislikes. He has His own set of attributes and preferences. He also knows us better than we know ourselves. Therefore, when we pray and talk with Him, He communicates with us according to what He knows is best. He might say yes to some of our requests; other times, He might say no. At times, it might not even seem like He is saying anything at all. But, to the Christian, God is always there, always taking care of us and always listening when we speak to Him. The theology of New Age spirituality cannot lead people to the Father who made them because it presents a notion of God that is no more personal than a microwave.

The Chaos Dragon Leviathan Compared Against the New Age Force

Strangely enough, the writers of the Bible did believe and describe a type of "force" in reality, but it was seen completely different from what New Age teaches today. In the ancient Near East, there was an understood personification of the impersonal force of chaos. The ancients called it Leviathan.[48] This entity was seen as a type of sea dragon even though it personified something that was impersonal. In ancient times, the seas were associated with chaos because they were dangerous and deadly. There were land-beast personifications of this as well, since chaos is not limited to the sea.

There were other names for this force and similar entities to Leviathan, depending on the region and ancient text, including Litanu, Lotan, Behemoth, Tiamat, Mot, Seth-Horus, and Cerberus, etc. The Enuma Elish is the Babylonian epic of creation describing the birth of the gods, the universe, and human beings.[49] In the beginning, according to the story, nothing existed except chaotic water everywhere. Out of the movement of the waters, they divided into fresh water and saltwater. The fresh water is personified as the god Apsu while the salt water is personified as the goddess Tiamat. Through these two entities came the birth of younger gods.

---

[48] "Jewishencyclopedia.Com." LEVIATHAN AND BEHEMOTH - JewishEncyclopedia.com. Accessed February 24, 2025. https://www.jewishencyclopedia.com/articles/9841-leviathan-and-behemoth.

[49] Mark, Joshua J. "Enuma Elish - the Babylonian Epic of Creation - Full Text." World History Encyclopedia, December 6, 2022. https://www.worldhistory.org/article/225/enuma-elish---the-babylonian-epic-of-creation---fu/.

The younger gods were noisy and were troubling Apsu, so he decided to kill the younger gods. Tiamat heard of this and warned her eldest son, Enki (sometimes Ea), who then killed Apsu. Tiamat became angry over Apsu's death, summoned the forces of chaos, and created eleven monsters to destroy the younger gods. Ea/Enki and the other younger gods fought against Tiamat but were unable to win the battle until Marduk emerged as a champion among them. Marduk killed Tiamat by shoot- ing her with an arrow, splitting her in two. Marduk created the heavens and the earth from Tiamat's corpse (half to make the heavens, half to make the earth). He then appointed jobs to the younger gods and bound Tiamat's eleven monsters to his feet as trophies.

Marduk then talked with Ea, recognized as the god of wisdom, and decided to create human beings. Ea created Lullu, the first man. Lullu's job was to help the gods in their task of maintaining order and restraining chaos. The story ends with a long praise of Marduk for everything he did. The entire story is about chaos being subdued by the destruction of a great sea beast. In other words, the sea beast is a symbol for chaos.

A similar story can be found in the Ugaritic Baal Cycle.[50] Ugarit was an ancient city located at what is now Ras Shamra in northern Syria. The Baal Cycle isn't as much about creation as it is about a competition between gods for a position of rulership with the supreme god El. It describes a battle between Baal ("lord") and Yam ("sea") and another battle between Baal and Mot ("death"). Yam is also called Nahar ("river") and is also described as a sea monster with seven heads named Litanu (the Canaanite word for 'Leviathan"). In the Baal Cycle, Yam is a symbol for the sea and the forces of chaos, comparable to Tiamat in the Enuma Elish. Baal defeated Yam and was declared king of the other gods, yet he was still under El. He was given the titles "the Rider on the Clouds," "Most High," and was described as having everlasting dominion.

As we can see, the cultures in the Ancient Near East personified chaos as a sea beast, sometimes with a land beast counterpart. They understood that the universe itself was pervaded with a non-living, yet very real, chaotic force, one that we needed divine protection against. The basic idea behind this was to answer the questions: Why do bad things

---

50 Smith, Mark S. "The Ugaritic Baal Cycle: Volume I." Logos Bible Software, January 1, 1994. https://www.logos.com/product/17888/the-ugaritic-baal-cycle-volume-i.

happen in the world? What is chaos and why does it exist? As stated in the Bible, especially in the Book of Job, the answer is that, while chaos/Leviathan is subdued, it is not yet vanquished, but will be when God deems it time to restore all of creation to Edenic conditions. Chaos entered the world when sin did. The main point is that, yes, the world is chaotic and yes, bad things happen to good people, but God ultimately is in control and does not allow chaos to have full reign over the planet.

The Book of Job is a great source of information to help answer this type of question. When Job questioned God and essentially suggested He should be running things differently, God challenged Job with a series of questions. This is where we are introduced to Behemoth, the personification of chaos on land:

Behold, Behemoth, which I made as I made you; he eats grass like an ox. Behold, his strength in his loins, and his power in the muscles of his belly. He makes his tail stiff like a cedar; the sinews of his thighs are knit together. His bones are tubes of bronze, his limbs like bars of iron. He is the first of the works of God; let him who made him bring near his sword! For the mountains yield food for him where all the wild beasts play. Under the lotus plants he lies, in the shelter of the reeds and in the marsh. For his shade the lotus trees cover him; the willows of the brook surround him. Behold, if the river is turbulent he is not frightened; he is confident though Jordan rushes against his mouth. Can one take him by his eyes, or pierce his nose with a snare? (Job 40:15–24)

Next, we are introduced to Leviathan, the personified sea beast of chaos:

Can you draw out Leviathan with a fishhook or press down his tongue with a cord? Can you put a rope in his nose or pierce his jaw with a hook? Will he make many pleas to you? Will he speak to you soft words? Will he make a covenant with you to take him for your servant forever? Will you play with him as with a bird, or will you put him on a leash for your girls? Will traders bargain over him? Will they divide him up among the merchants? Can you fill his skin with harpoons or his head with fishing spears? Lay your hands on him; remember the battle— you will not do it again! Behold, the hope of a man is false; he is laid low even at the sight of him. No one is so fierce that he dares to stir him up. Who then is he who can stand before me? Who has first given to me, that I should repay him? Whatever is under the whole heaven is mine. I will *not keep silence concerning his limbs, or his mighty strength, or his goodly frame. Who can strip off his outer garment? Who would come near him with a bridle? Who can open the doors of his face? Around his teeth is terror. His back is made of rows of shields, shut up closely as with a seal. One is so near to another that no air can come between them. They are joined one to another; they clasp each other and cannot be separated. His sneezings flash forth light, and his eyes are like the eyelids of the dawn. Out of his mouth go flaming torches; sparks of fire leap forth. Out of his nostrils comes forth smoke, as from a boiling pot and burning rushes. His breath kindles coals, and a flame comes forth from his mouth. In his neck abides strength, and terror dances before him. The folds of his flesh stick together, firmly cast on him and immovable. His heart is hard as a stone, hard as the lower mill- stone. When he raises himself up, the mighty are afraid; at the crashing they are beside themselves. Though the sword reaches him, it does not avail, nor the spear, the dart, or the javelin. He counts iron as straw, and bronze as rotten wood. The arrow can- not make him flee; for him, sling stones are turned to stubble. Clubs are counted as stubble; he laughs at the rattle of javelins. His underparts are like sharp potsherds; he spreads himself like a threshing sledge on the mire. He makes the deep boil like a pot; he makes the sea like a pot of ointment. Behind him he leaves a shining wake; one would think the deep to be white-haired. On earth there is not his like, a creature without fear. He sees everything that is high; he is king over all the sons of pride. (Job 41)*

God makes the point that Job is unable to even face Leviathan and Behemoth. Job, who is mortal and not eternal, does not know enough about spiritual and physical reality to question God's reasonings. Instead of questioning, therefore, Job should trust that God knows what He's doing and understand there is information he doesn't have about the nature of chaos within creation. It is the same for us today.

When tragedy occurs, such as mass shootings, hurricanes, and other such things, they are expressions of chaos (sometimes including intelligent evil, such as in the cases of mass shootings). However, while the chaos itself is antagonistic and hostile to humanity, God is ultimately sovereign over the chaos. We don't have to fear it because God subdues chaos. Even more, Scripture tells us what we can do in light of these tragedies, such as praying and loving one another, and this does not include giving all our attention to the terror of Leviathan while disregarding the power of the Almighty.

While ancient cultures understood the universe to be permeated with an impersonal force of chaos that threatened our existence, the New Age takes a different approach and sees this impersonal force as something to be incorporated into one's spirituality. They assume, naively, that the background force radiating into the created world must be benevolent and life-giving, even though the universe is a chaotic, death-filled place. Instead, New Agers fully embrace the "energy of the universe" without a second thought to what kind of energy they might be embracing. However, the danger, if the biblical description is correct, is that New Age believers might inadvertently be tapping into the energy or force of chaos that entered creation at the Fall, perhaps even the same one modern science says responsible for the gradual decline and disorder of all things in the universe (entropy).

What if the energy force we are connecting with is the same one the ancients were terrified of, and the same one causing death, decay, and degradation in the natural world? A simple practice such as meditation can open a door for chaos to enter one's life. This is exactly what happened to me. While my experience was more a spiritual manifestation of chaos, it might not always come about that way. Chaos could come in unrecognizable form to humans living in a fallen world. If we get hurt, a loved one gets sick, we lose our job, or we go through divorce, we don't typically see these things as anything more than what life usually has to offer. What if that's not the end of the story?

What if there is a reason these events occur to some people at certain times rather than others? What if there is something we humans are doing to invite the old chaos dragon into our lives?

The New Age movement is in the business of bringing people into contact with the impersonal energy force of the universe, not considering that the universe is a chaos-driven and has been understood to be such by the same cultures its adherents so highly revere. The Apostle Paul understood that all forces of destruction have their origin in the god of this world (2 Corinthians 4:4), whom he calls the prince of the power of the air (Ephesians 2:2).

Leviathan and the chaos it represents belong to the dominion of Satan, who brought death and chaos into the world through sin. We should not assume that, just because we are in touch with an impersonal force in the universe, this force is benevolent or from a benevolent source. The Bible tells us that at least one impersonal universal force is destructive (Leviathan) and comes from a malevolent source (Satan). It also tells us to avoid practices that bring us into contact force (such as mediation, trance, chanting, and drugs, etc.), as these practices bring us not only into contact with the force itself (which opens the door for chaos to enter our lives), but also with the personal spiritual forces overseeing such practices (Ephesians 6:12)—making it doubly dangerous.

Those in the New Age movement are obsessed with trying to connect with the impersonal forces of nature, not realizing that the impersonal forces of nature were understood by the ancients to be so chaotic as to be personified in the form of sea monsters and dragons that threatened the survival of the human race.

If science, the Bible, and the Mediterranean world reveal that chaos is the universal force fueling cosmic goings on, perhaps the New Age practice of tapping into the impersonal forces of the universe is an invitation to destruction.

Strangely enough, while many New Agers recognize an impersonal force that drives the entire universe, there is still a belief in other spiritual beings. These spiritual beings are not malevolent like the dragon of chaos, of course. They are understood as benevolent. Many times, these beings are seen as making up a hierarchy with a pantheon of powerful beings at the top. This pantheon consists of personal beings rather than impersonal forces; however, the overall impersonal force still drives everything at a fundamental level.

Now that we have identified the enemy, their practices, and how to defend against them, we can look to some more positive aspects of prophecy and the supernatural. What can we as Christians expect in the future? We know what is ultimately in store for the enemy (utter destruction), but what will we experience?

Part 4: Signs in Eternity: The Future for Believers

Chapter 19: The Dead Sea Scrolls Rapture

For those new to this subject, I'll just give a very brief synopsis of what the Dead Sea Scrolls are. During the time of Jesus, there were three main schools of thought on how to interpret the Old Testament. The Pharisees had what they called "oral torah," which were oral traditions passed down through time to interpret the Torah and they believed prophecy had ceased in their time. The Sadducees got to a point where they didn't believe in much of anything, including angels or the afterlife. Then there were the Essenes, who followed the teachings of the Zadok Priests, and they were the writers and keeps of the Dead Sea Scrolls in Qumran.

The Essenes believed they held onto the original teachings of Judaism in how it was always meant to be followed from the Old Testament. One of those teachings was their solar calendar which they said was the same one God gave to Adam. The Pharisees and Sadducees, by contrast, had adopted a pagan lunar calendar a couple hundred years before the time of Christ.[51]

The Dead Sea Scroll calendar fits perfectly with the Bible. You can use this calendar from Genesis to Revelation and it all works. Even more than a yearly calendar, they also had an understanding of the totality of creation, from the first day of creation until the last day before the New Heavens and New Earth, as lasting for exactly 7,000 years, modeled after the calendar week. They split up this time in many ways, but most notably there are four ages, the first three lasting 2,000 years each, and the last age is a 1,000-year Sabbath Rest. We would understand that as the Millennial Reign.

The first age, called the Age of Creation, or sometimes the Age of Chaos, lasted between the first day of Creation and the call of Abraham. The second Age, called the Torah Age, lasted

---

[51] For more information, check out my two-volume book set *Forgotten Prophecies of the Dead Sea Scrolls* available at ProphecyWatchers.com

between the call of Abraham and 76 AD, a few years after the temple was destroyed. The third Age, called the Age of Grace, began in 76 AD and, according to the calendar, is set to end in 2076 AD. Then the final age would be between 2076 and 3076 AD. That means that the final jubilee, meaning 50 years, of our age is set to begin in 2026. So, again, the question comes up, if we have this 50 year span until the start of the Millennial Reign, and we know we have a rapture, 7-year tribulation, and return of Christ before the Millennial Reign can begin, then do we have to wait until 2068 or 2069 for the rapture? That would be a pretty depressing thought, but thankfully, that's not the only way this could play out.

First off, it's important to note that the rapture is not the event that begins the tribulation. Daniel 9:27 states:

"Then he shall confirm a covenant with many for one week; But in the middle of the week He shall bring an end to sacrifice and offering. And on the wing of abominations shall be one who makes desolate, Even until the consummation, which is determined, Is poured out on the desolate."

The beginning of the tribulation begins with the confirmation of a covenant with "many," which actually refers to Israel, and that "one week" is actually a shemitah which is a period of seven years. By this point, the rapture would have already happened. We don't know how long of a period of time there is between the rapture and the start of the tribulation. Years could have passed.

Now there's a really good objection to this theory will I'll address in a moment, but just to explain, technically there could even be decades between the rapture and the start of the tribulation. So, just for sake of argument and not setting dates, let's say you have the rapture in 2026. There's nothing spelled out specifically in the Bible that would prohibit the start of the tribulation still occurring in 2069. Also, imagine how much deception the world would be thrown in if it were to happen that way.

The rapture comes, seven years go by and no prophecies have been fulfilled: no Antichrist, no cosmic signs, no return of Jesus. Well, in a scenario like that, those people who accepted Christ right after the rapture would start to appear pretty silly to nonbelievers. Now imagine a couple decades go by. At this time, you have a whole generation of people born in a past-rapture world who, not having lived through it, wouldn't have he same perspective or respect for it that those who did would. Could this be why, all throughout Revelation, people have such a hard time converting and believing what they are seeing with their own eyes? There's a lot more to it than that, but that's the basic idea of the theory.

Now, there is a good objection to this, and I heard this first from my good friend Mondo Gonzales, that basically says we are given two examples of what to expect: Noah and Lot. In both of those cases, God rescued them right before the destruction came. God didn't put Noah on the ark decades before the flood came and God didn't rescue Lot decades before the fire and brimstone came. So, following that pattern, it's most likely the rapture will occur just before the tribulation starts. I think that is a really good point and one we should definitely keep in mind. One could say that God warned Noah 120 years before the flood that it was going to happen and began giving him instructions for his escape at that time, but Noah was still on Earth, not in the ark, and we don't have anything like that with Lot, so the fact that God warned Noah early doesn't correlate in my opinion. So, are we back to having to wait until 2068 or 2069 for the rapture? Not necessarily, there is still another option.

We know in the final jubilee of the Age of Torah, which began in 25 or 26 AD, Jesus fulfilled the prophecies of His first coming very early. He was crucified in 32 AD, only 7 years or one shemitah into the final jubilee. We as Christians would say that our Age of Grace started with the indwelling of the Holy Spirit, which is true. But think of it as a piece of the next age that was brought in as a precursor to when the next age would officially start.

Think of it this way; I could say I'm going to throw a birthday party next Friday at 3:00pm. Well, in order to prepare for that, I might schedule the attractions on Tuesday, order the cake on Wednesday, buy the gifts on Thursday, and pick up the cake on Friday at 1pm, so that by Friday at 3pm, everything is ready and in place. It could even be that I had everything ready an in place an hour before the party was set to start, but would we say that the party really started at 2pm? No, even if people started showing up early, we'd still say the official start of the party is at 3pm. Ages work in a similar way. There was a lot that needed to happen before the official Age of Grace could begin, including the destruction of the temple and the abolishment of the Pharisaical sacrificial system. Similarly, we have a lot that needs to happen before the Millennial Reign can officially begin, and it's more than just the rapture and tribulation.

It could stand to reason that we could have an early rapture, tribulation, and return of Jesus in our final jubilee. So again, let's just say for sake of argument and not trying to set dates, just using this as an example, that the rapture occurs in 2025. Shortly after, the covenant is confirmed and the tribulation begins. Let's say that Jesus then returns in 2032 (which is interesting because that would be exactly 2,000 years after He was crucified, resurrected, and ascended into Heaven). In this example, much how Jesus fulfilled the prophecies of His first coming early in the final Jubilee but there was still a temple and an old system to deal with, Jesus could do the same thing in our age. He could fulfill the prophecies about his second coming early in our final jubilee. Of course, this begs the question, what will everyone be doing then between the years of 2032 and 2075 while we wait for the Millennial Reign to officially begin. Well, much like the end of the Torah Age, we still have a temple and an old system to deal with.

The last few chapters of the book of Ezekiel give us a lot of detail on how things will work in the Millennium. Ezekiel is shown an amazing temple and a beautifully immense city. He's also given specific measurements of everything so we know this is literal and is most definitely not figurative language. By the time Ezekiel sees this, everything is already built and functioning. But, we must ask, how long did it take to build the new temple and the city? Many people assume that when Jesus returns He will snap his fingers and everything will be different, but there really isn't any reason to think that's the case. Isaiah 2:4 states:

"And he shall judge among the nations, and shall rebuke many people: and they shall beat their swords into plowshares, and their spears into pruninghooks: nation shall not lift up sword against nation, neither shall they learn war any more."

Notice the progression of events in this verse. First, the nations are judged. We read about that in other places as well, but after Jesus comes back and defeats the Antichrist, He judges the nations. We don't know exactly how long that judgment will take. After that, it's the people themselves that beat their swords into plowshares. Jesus doesn't snap his fingers and transform the swords into plowshares. People do that physical work themselves. It stands to reason that it will be people, under the direction of Jesus, who build the new temple and the city. How long might that take? Well, interestingly enough, the rebuilding of the Second Temple by Herod the Great stared in 20 BC and lasted for 46 years. A project like that can easily take decades. Adding to that, how long does it take to instruct the whole world on how things are going to play out now? The Age of Grace will be ending, so much like how when the Age of Torah was ending, instructions will have to go out to the world to teach everyone what Jesus expects from now on and how everything will be conducted. How long could that take? Given all this, it is entirely possible that we could have an early rapture, tribulation, and return of Jesus but then still have a few decades of "clean up" before, just like the birthday party example, everything is in place and ready to officially begin the Millennial Reign of Christ and the final 1,000 year Sabbath of all of Creation before the New Heavens and New Earth.

Of course, all of this is speculative and we just don't know for sure how everything will pan out, but I wanted to explain how we can have 50 years left but that we don't necessarily need to wait all that time for anything to happen. The rapture could happen at any time, so make sure you're ready, we're already seeing things getting insane in the world and I think we kind of all feel like there's not much time left, so look up, for our redemption draws near.

Chapter 20: Future Bodies of Believers

There are, of course, many books about Heaven and the resurrected bodies people who have given their lives to Christ in their physical lives will receive. However, there are very few books in mainstream Christianity that clearly identify the need for this body and how we can understand the attributes this body will need in order to fulfill the promises of God. Some things are clearly laid out in scripture while others require some thought. There are easy things that are talked about in most Christian books on the topic. For example, if the resurrection of Jesus is an example of what we can expect, we know our glorified bodies will be able to walk through walls, will have some kind of structure such as bones, will be able to eat (Luke 24:36-43), can fly (Acts 1:9), will be immortal (1 Corinthians 15:53-55), etc. However these are just things on the surface.

The true purpose for and attributes of our resurrected bodies is far more glorious than we could ever imagine, yet it is almost never discussed in mainstream Christianity. I believe this is because the topic can get very deep and complex. While this is impossible to avoid, I will try my best to explain these complexities in this chapter. I will also attempt to explain the same concepts using different examples and methods since again, they can be a bit difficult.

The Philosophy of Resurrection

Much could be said and, indeed, has been written on what the Bible says about the resurrection and our glorified bodies. In any book addressing the afterlife from a Christian perspective, these things cannot be ignored. However, instead of rehashing the common things that have already been written in countless Christian books, I want to focus on some lesser known aspects of eternity, resurrection, and our future, glorified bodies.

The Christian doctrine of resurrection has received a lot of attentions from philosophers. We Christians believe the resurrection of Jesus serves as a model of what we can expect if we have submitted to Jesus and became born again believers. We believe people who rejected Jesus will be resurrected as well, but it will be for judgment rather than reward. In Acts 24:15b, Paul says *"...that there will be a resurrection of both the just and the unjust."*

Materialist and Immaterialist philosophers have been debating the resurrection for quite some time. In what's been called "the simulacra model," Peter van Inwagen attempts to present a model of resurrection that is compatible with materials and the Christian doctrine of resurrection. The problem for the materialist who is trying to defend resurrection as described by Christianity is that the body begins to break down and become destroyed by natural processes after death. Van Inwagen's solution is to propose a model of resurrection in which our physical bodies do not decay, but instead are replaced with a copy called a "simulacrum." He stated *"at the moment of each man's death, God removes his corpse and replaces it with a simulacrum, which is what is burned or rots."*[52] Then, at the time of the resurrection, God will take the preserved corpse and restore it to life.

There are obvious problems to this, even for materialists. Van Ingwen even admits in this article that there is no reason for God to replace a corpse with a simulacrum. God could just as well remove and preserve our corpses and not replace it with anything at all. Van Inwagen attempts to give an answer by saying if God did not replace corpses with simulacra, there would be widespread and irrefutable proof of the existence of the supernatural. Van Inwagen even admits in a postscript to his original article:

I am inclined now to think of the description that I gave in 'The Possibility of Resurrection' of how an omnipotent being could accomplish the Resurrection of the Dead as a 'just-so story': Although it serves to establish a possibility, it probably isn't true.[53]

Of the immaterialist views on resurrection, Augustine's and Aquinas' are probably among the most popular. Augustine

---

[52] Inwagen, Peter Van. "The Possibility of Resurrection" and Other Essays in Christian Apologetics. Boulder, CO: Westview Press, 1999.

[53] Ibid.

was an early adopter of a form of dualism inspired by Plato and Descartes, which stated:

- The body and the soul are separate substances.
- The soul is immaterial.
- The soul is identical or strongly connected to the mind.

Augustine added to this that the soul is immortal. He argued the soul must be immortal because it desires perfect happiness, and no happiness would be perfect if one feared losing it at death. Thomas Aquinas held the view that people are a substance that is a blend of both matter and form. This substantial form is the rational soul. This is called the "hylomorphic" view. There was a debate between people who held this view about whether or not the soul could survive death and, if it could, whether or not this would ensure a personal resurrection. Aquinas argued that the human mind/soul can exist apart from the physical body. The mind/soul doesn't depend on the physical body for existence. Therefore, instead of just ceasing to exist at physical death, when the soul becomes disembodied it would come to know the world in a different way. Aquinas also argued that we can expect a personal resurrection.

This shows that even in ancient times, philosophers, theologians, and religious thinkers understood the importance of a resurrection. But why do we need a resurrection at all? We know God promises it will happen in the Bible, but if our soul can detach from our physical body and live on with God, what need do we have for a resurrection and glorification of the physical body? These are very good questions with some very complicated answers. The key to the need for resurrection is understanding the need of the spirit for embodiment.

The Need For Embodiment

Here is something interesting to think about and will lay the framework of this chapter: Every time God interacts with man or angel, He is embodied to some degree. There is a difference between physical embodiment and spiritual embodiment. God is never described as some disembodied essence. For example, when He interacts with men or angels, He speaks. Why is this?

It is entirely possible that any kind of communion with God is impossible unless it is done through some type of embodiment. Think about what God actually is. Is He he physical form as Jesus Christ on Earth? Yes, not not entirely. Is God His heavenly embodiment as the King on the throne? Yes, though again, not entirely. Is God truly His Holy essence in whatever that means for Him in His own subjective sense? Yes! This is because God's own subjective sense of Himself is the ultimate objective reality. No one can truly know that purely objective truth but God Himself because He is One and there are none like Him. This means, all of creation, from the highest angel to the lowliest worm, can only interact with God through a type of means that, in a sense, filters His own subjective/objective nature in a way we can understand. But, included with that is the embodiment, which is why God is typically understood as a trinity. God decided to create man, meaning God had a desire that was fulfilled in His creation of us, meaning that included with that would have to be a way for Him to interact and have a relationship with us, meaning the trinity is absolutely necessary. Yet, we know God was/is a trinity even before He created man. Therefore, the means by which God can interact with us, angels, and anything else He created was in place before anything else outside of God Himself existed.

This can be very confusing and, if one is not careful, can lead someone to believe all of creation is equal to God because of these things, but this is not so because of one missing element: time. God is eternal and time is His creation. This means God exists both outside of and within time. Eternity is a state of being outside of time. Temporal is a state of being within time. There was a "time" (for lack of better word) before time was created. That statement isn't accurate technically, but it does show the limitations of human language. Naturally, anything God creates would have to be less than Him. A creation of God certainly couldn't be greater because God is the greatest; nothing could be conceived of that is greater than God otherwise that would be God. Nothing can exist without being created by God, as we looked at in the last chapter. No creation of God can be equal with God, because then God would not be One. Therefore, everything God created is less, or more limited, than Him.

Think for a moment of the makeup of a human being. A human is body, soul, and spirit. The spirit is the thing that we really are; it's the thing that animates the rest. The spirit is the subjective understanding of one's own self. God modeled us after Himself, yet limited. God too has a body (Jesus), soul (heavenly Father on the throne), and spirit (or "Holy Spirit," God's own ultimate subjective understanding of Himself, which is the ultimate truth be cause nothing could be truer, therefore it is also the ultimate objective truth), and all of these are God. It's not exactly accurate to say they are pieces of God, because they are all fully God. It is similar to say ice, water, and steam are all fully H2O, yet this isn't a perfect analogy (mainly because there is no such thing as a perfect analogy, they all break down at some point) because these are still different states of existence based on temperature.

Because we are lesser, we would never be able to interact with God without the limiting factor of embodiment. I say "limiting" based on just our own perspective, because embodiment doesn't "limit" God, just like it doesn't "enhance" Him either. God is already the ultimate and the infinite; there is no taking away or adding to God. Yet, from our own already-limited perspective, we can see how we cannot fully appreciate God Himself in His entirety without us being equal to God, which again is impossible. This is why Jesus Christ is necessary and why everything points back to Him. Without Him, in every sense, we could never truly be reconciled to God.

Going back to time, we must understand that we are not who are right now in this moment in time. In the same way, we are not only our body, soul, or spirit. To be truly who we are meant to be the way God intends it, we must be all three; but again, not merely all three in one moment of time. We are not who we are today, but we are the totality of who we are in every moment of time, including eternity if we have given our lives to Jesus. The totality of who we are is body, soul, and spirit in and out of all moments in time. Within the totality of time, we only exist physically in a part of it. However, in eternity, outside of time, we just are.

The amazing thing is this trinitarian attribute of God preexisted human beings. Yet is God was only spirit, we would have no way to tangibly interact with Him, meaning His desire to create human beings and angels would not truly be fulfilled, which means He wouldn't be all powerful, and the whole concept breaks apart. However, if God was already a trinity before He created man, the aspects and attributes of His very nature always included the creation of mankind. It means that creating man wasn't merely a desire for God in the way we would think of it. A desire of God's is actually a necessity, because how could and all powerful God have a desire that does not end up fulfilled? Therefore, because He desired to create mankind, mankind was a necessity by the very nature of God.

I bring this up because human words cannot possible truly explain what God's love for us really means. It goes beyond love. We can't really grasp how important we are to God. We also can't grasp how important things like free will, justice, perfection, and others are to God. We can't truly grasp how much of a waste it is to ignore these things throughout life and reject God entirely. We are not God, therefore we cannot truly ever understand God the way He understands Himself. We can know Him, of course, if we don't waste the gift He's given us in Jesus Christ. We can interact with Him. But it is necessary for there, again, to be a type of means we can perceive Him through. This means is embodiment.

This is why a physical body, a spiritual body, and a physical resurrection of the body which becomes a glorified body is needed. Without it, we have no way of perceiving God. We would be disembodied spirits with no possible means through which to interact with God. In other words, we would be completely separated from God in every way imaginable. Without right standing with God, we are just consciousnesses without any kind of housing, blind and deaf, completely separated from the only thing that makes us whole; we are the absolute personification of incomplete, we only know nothing but pain in every sense because no good can come without God. We are, in a sense, worse than nothing.

We know there is a future resurrection and we will have physical bodies that can interact in both the physical and spiritual worlds; on Earth and in Heaven. You might ask, why do we need a body that can interact with the physical world at all? Once we're dead, isn't getting to go to Heaven enough? The answer is, it is a matter of being "whole" and "restored." You cannot be fully restored if you don't have access to a place you once had access to. This is why the body of the resurrected and glorified Christ was able to move about freely in our three dimensions of space, but was also able to move freely in higher dimensions, which is how He could ascend to the clouds and enter an apparently closed room.

This very well might be why a resurrection is required in order for things to truly be restored. Without a glorified and resurrected body, Jesus may not have had the same type of three-three-dimensional perspective, meaning He may not have been able to interact or communicate with the physical world at all. To truly be restored, glorified, and have access to all God has created, we need not only an extradimensional soul, but a physical resurrection of the body. This new body is not subject to death, deterioration, or decay, but is immortal.

When Do We Receive Our New Bodies?

Most Christians believe when we die, we are temporarily in our extradimensional soul awaiting a resurrected body. You might wonder, why don't we see people who have died interacting with this physical world? Why was the glorified Jesus so much different than what we would think of as a ghost? We have to remember, the judgment has not taken place yet. People who rejected Christ have not yet been consigned to the second death in the lake of fire. It is reasonable to assume, from our perspective as physical beings, our dead loved ones who accepted Christ do not yet have their glorified bodies.

Glorified Bodies and Eternity

There is obviously a difference between how we see time and how God sees it. It seems, by everything the Bible says on the matter, that God is outside of time and can see all points in time (past, present, and future) at once. This might help explain one of the most enigmatic verses in all the Bible concerning our future with Jesus. Ephesians 2:5-6:

4 But God, being rich in mercy, because of the great love with which he loved us,5 even when we were dead in our trespasses, made us alive together with Christ—by grace you have been saved— 6 and raised us up with him and seated us with him in the heavenly places in Christ Jesus, 7 so that in the coming ages he might show the immeasurable riches of his grace in kindness toward us in Christ Jesus.

The clear message here is that God loves us so much. However, there is more here. Notice the use of past and future tense in this passage. Many times, when this passage is interpreted, it is taught that Jesus sees us as if we are already seated with Him. However, the text teaches this principal in past tense, portraying the fact that this has already happened. When we were dead, He made us alive together with Christ, and raised us up, and seated us together in the heavenly places in Christ Jesus. If we have accepted Jesus as our Savior, this is already done.

When we look at this passage closely, we realize very direct and literal language is used. We do not see as if or like anywhere in the passage. It is directly saying that a literal event occurred when you and I accepted Jesus Christ as our Savior. We were literally seated in Heaven with Jesus.

The Greek word used for the idea of us being raised together comes from "synegeirō", meaning:

"1. to raise together, to cause to raise together

2. to raise up together from mortal death to a new and blessed life dedicated to God."[54]

From this, we can realize that we were, in a sense, born into death, but since we accepted Jesus' gift of salvation, we have been raised and seated in Heaven. Also notice that this happened to all of us together, implicating that it happened within the same instant.

What we are dealing with here is the same event in two different understandings of time; one within and one without. This is why understanding eternity as a state outside of time can help us. In the one linear dimension of time we can experience here on Earth, we accept Jesus as our Savior and

[54] "Greek Lexicon :: G4891 (KJV)." Blue Letter Bible. Accessed 24 July, 2019. http://www.blueletterbible.org/lang/Lexicon/Lexicon.cfm?Strongs=G4891&t=KJV

begin our new life. To God in eternity, this reality just is. The passage seems to be saying that we as Christians are already in Heaven, at least as far as God in eternity is concerned. Right now, as you are reading this, if you are secure in Jesus, you are already seated with Jesus in Heaven from God's perspective. Now, of course, this is something outside of the physical timeline. We cannot apply this to our physical lives and think we can do whatever we want because it is already done in eternity. We still have free will. We still have a choice. We can still choose to accept or reject Jesus.

Before accepting Jesus' gift of salvation, we lived our lives in sin and death. If we had continued down that path and had never accepted Jesus, we would be dead already spiritually, even though we would still be physically alive. That is what the beginning of the passage in Ephesians is signifying. Accepting the gift of salvation takes us out of the spiritual state of death and raises us to life with Jesus Christ outside of knowable time and space. This is what it means to be born again. You're born once into a physical body of death and you must be born again in spirit into a body of incorruptible perfection that can exist in eternity.

As the passage suggests, when we accepted Jesus, we were lifted into eternity, outside of knowable time and space, to be seated with Jesus where we are now. In a sense, this seems to convey the idea that we are in two places at once, though we would not normally realize it without revelation from God through the Bible. However, thinking of "two places at once" isn't exactly accurate. This would only be from God's perspective. It would be more accurate to say that God sees and interacts with us at every point in time simultaneously.

Another interesting thing to note about this passage is it says we were raised together. This also adds to the theory of us already being there from God's perspective. Because God is outside of knowable time (yet also within it), when I was saved and when you were saved, we were raised together, even if we were saved years apart. We were also raised together with the apostle Paul when he accepted Jesus as his Savior.

In linear time, we can point to a specific time when we were saved. However, on the other side from God's perspective, it is all the same and we share in it together. In other words, we are already in Heaven, but not yet. This shows us even more of the sheer beauty and majesty of our

Lord Almighty. There is no way any of us will fully understand the depths of this concept until it is time for us to escape our own physical existence. It will be then when each one of us who have found our salvation in Jesus Christ will wake up together, and like coming out of a long a terrifying dream, we will realize in utter relief and joy that we have been with Jesus all along.

Conclusion: Signs in Love

We have finally reached the end and there is one more amazing aspect of the supernatural I would like to discuss. To preface that, I have a confession. Years ago (long before working in full time ministry) I was an internet troll. Back then that term wasn't developed yet, but I was one of them. I wouldn't have thought of myself that way, of course. To me, I was practicing tough love on ignorant Christians who should have known better about their theology. After all, if there wasn't all of these wrong ideas, I wouldn't have to spend so much time and frustration on Facebook, right?

Well, that's how I would justify it to myself, at least. Of course, as I know now thanks to God, I was horribly wrong. My behaviors were rooted in pride and not at all in scripture (even though I was extremely good at twisting scripture to suit my emotional needs). Not only that, but my judgment of others was way off. If I came across a person online who didn't share my personal interpretations of scripture or theology, I would come to the conclusion they must not be a real Christian. Or, if they were, they certainly weren't walking closely with the Lord. After all, if they were, they would share the same rapture belief, view on extra-biblical books, and interpretation of end-times prophecy as me.

I also made sure to let them know it. I would spend countless hours in threads hundreds of comments long just to argue my point. Not pleasantly and politely inform others of my beliefs while giving validation to theirs, mind you. I'm talking outright fighting tooth and nail to bust my opponent's opinions down while elevating mine as high as scripture itself. It is amazing, looking back, not only how obviously wrong I was in my approach, but how I totally didn't see it. I was the one who wasn't walking closely with the Lord. I was only walking closely with myself: my beliefs, my opinions, and my interpretations held priority over everything else.

Later, after God had prepared my heart for it, He brought various people through my life who (over the course of years) unknowingly helped me confront my pride issue and humble myself to the Lord. This, of course, came at a cost. I had to give up the idea that I had all the answers. I had to give up the idea that my walk with God was fine how it was. I had to totally abolish the idea that I was not a prideful person. A new path had been set before me.

Over the course of time and a lot of hard work, God showed me how I was actually hurting myself and others with the way I chose to behave online. I realized I wasn't viewing people online as real people, but more as random faceless names who had no bearing on the real world through my own perception. I treated people online totally different than how I treated people in real life. If someone spoke to me in person, for the most part they were left with the impression of me as a very kind and polite individual. I was not. However, I was really good at hiding it because in the real world, unlike the internet (or so I thought), there is accountability. If things get heated in person, you're in it until it comes to some sort of resolution. Online, however, you always have the option of blocking someone, turning off the computer, or worse yet, continuing in increasingly heated arguments until the other person gives up.

The obvious problem: I was not living by the Word. The Bible, believe it or not, has a lot to say about loving one another despite petty differences. The things I used to be upset abut in other people were not salvation issue; yet I learned, even if they were, it still would not excuse my behavior. We are absolutely commanded to operate out of love: love for God and love for one another.

I used to think I was operating out of love for God. If I didn't love Him, I wouldn't defend Him so fervently, right? Only I was operating from my definition of love, not the Bible's. 1 John 4:20-21 states:

20 If anyone says, "I love God," and hates his brother, he is a liar; for he who does not love his brother whom he has seen cannot love God whom he has not seen. 21 And this commandment we have from him: whoever loves God must also love his brother.

Going along with that, Galatians 5:13-15 states:

13 For you were called to freedom, brothers. Only do not use your freedom as an opportunity for the flesh, but through love serve one another. 14 For the whole law is fulfilled in one word: *"You shall love your neighbor as yourself." 15 But if you bite and devour one another, watch out that you are not consumed by one another.*

The easy way out of this, of course (at least it would seem), is to assume because it says "brother", we can treat who we consider non-brothers in Christ however we want. We would be mistaken. Luke 6:27-31 states:

27 "But I say to you who hear, Love your enemies, do good to those who hate you, 28 bless those who curse you, pray for those who abuse you. 29 To one who strikes you on the cheek, offer the other also, and from one who takes away your cloak do not withhold your tunic either. 30 Give to everyone who begs from you, and from one who takes away your goods do not demand them back. 31 And as you wish that others would do to you, do so to them.

Romans 12:14-21 states:

14 Bless those who persecute you; bless and do not curse them. 15 Rejoice with those who rejoice, weep with those who weep. 16 Live in harmony with one another. Do not be haughty, but associate with the lowly. Never be wise in your own sight. 17 Repay no one evil for evil, but give thought to do what is honorable in the sight of all. 18 If possible, so far as it depends on you, live peaceably with all. 19 Beloved, never avenge yourselves, but leave it to the wrath of God, for it is written, "Vengeance is mine, I will repay, says the Lord." 20 To the contrary, "if your enemy is hungry, feed him; if he is thirsty, give him something to drink; for by so doing you will heap burning coals on his head." 21 Do not be overcome by evil, but overcome evil with good.

Overcome evil with good. This immediately removes us from any thinking that just because someone is doing evil, it gives us the right to bust them down for it. Absolutely not. We are to show them love like they've never seen before. Of course, when I was trolling, I should have known better. I had even read these passages. However, I breezed past them and didn't think about how to apply this into my life, especially online.

The main reason I bring all of this up is not only for a confessional. The same behaviors God rooted out of me, I see running rampant online in many Christian circles. Even more, it is troublesome because these people are self-professing followers of Jesus Christ and I have no reason to believe they aren't saved, meaning they are brothers and sisters in Christ and I love them. The thing is, I believe most people are doing these kinds of things online purely out of ignorance. For some reason or another, just like me years ago, they don't know better. I also believe they represent the minority of Christians at this point. However, they also have the loudest voice. Most Christians who do not wish to behave this way will bow out of the conversation, go to another page, block, delete, and never think of the trolls again. In many cases this is absolutely what should be done, but at the same time the majority of Christians need to, in a sense "troll" the haters. We need to write articles about brotherly love, share bible verses, teach lessons, and most importantly, we ourselves need to do all of this out of love and not out of condemnation.

We need to get to a point where we can honestly say to God we are sharing these things purely out of love for the other person and absolutely not out of love of being right. We are to love one another. We are to be the helpful big brother or sister assisting their younger siblings in the best ways to behave. We are not to be know-it-all tattlers who's only motivation is to prove to Dad how right we are by showing how wrong our brother and sisters are. No good earthly father would put up with that, and our Heavenly Father doesn't appreciate it either.

It's hard to love, it really is. True love, not just the appearance of it, is a learned skill perfected by practice. It's not easy. However, it's what our Father expects from us. Luke 6:32-36 states:

32 "If you love those who love you, what benefit is that to you? For even sinners love those who love them. 33 And if you do good to those who do good to you, what benefit is that to you? For even sinners do the same. 34 And if you lend to those from whom you expect to receive, what credit is that to you? Even sinners lend to sinners, to get back the same amount. 35 But love your enemies, and do good, and lend, expecting nothing in return, and your reward will be great, and you will be sons of the Most High, for he is kind to the ungrateful and the evil. 36 Be merciful, even as your Father is merciful.

Romans 12:9-13 states:

9 Let love be genuine. Abhor what is evil; hold fast to what is good. 10 Love one another with brotherly affection. Outdo one another in showing honor. 11 Do not be slothful in zeal, be fervent in spirit,[a] serve the Lord. 12 Rejoice in hope, be patient in tribulation, be constant in prayer. 13 Contribute to the needs of the saints and seek to show hospitality.

We are not called to be easily offended. We live in a nation, culture, and even world full of easily offended people. If you say the wrong thing or have the wrong idea, suddenly the other person is being persecuted and you are the abuser. Scripture teaches against this mentality. 1 Corinthians 4:12-13 states:

12 and we labor, working with our own hands. When reviled, we bless; when persecuted, we endure; 13 when slandered, we entreat. We have become, and are still, like the scum of the world, the refuse of all things.

To end with, we must all (myself included) remember, in all things, that love is absolutely most important. 1 Corinthians 13:1-8a states:

1 If I speak in the tongues of men and of angels, but have not love, I am a noisy gong or a clanging cymbal. 2 And if I have prophetic powers, and understand all mysteries and all knowledge, and if I have all faith, so as to remove mountains, but have not love, I am nothing. 3 If I give away all I have, and if I deliver up my body to be burned, but have not love, I gain nothing. 4 Love is patient and kind; love does not envy or boast; it is not arrogant 5 or rude. It does not insist on its own way; it is not irritable or resentful; 6 it does not rejoice at wrongdoing, but rejoices with the truth. 7 Love bears all things, believes all things, hopes all things, endures all things. 8 Love never ends.

Believe it or not, only 17 percent of Christians who consider their faith important and attend church regularly actually have a biblical worldview, according to Barna's research.[55] Shocking as that is on the surface, it really isn't too surprising once we consider all the variables. For example, we live in a totally connected world. The internet has made it possible for all people of all kinds to share their ideas. This would be a great thing if people valued personal discernment as much as sharing their own ideas. Unfortunately, this is not the case. One doesn't even have to be a great writer to convince anyone of anything; all one needs is an interesting idea that appeals to a person's sense of self-worth and importance.

---

[55] "Competing Worldviews Influence Today's Christians." Barna Group, June 27, 2023. https://www.barna.com/research/competing-worldviews-influence-todays-christians/.

Generally, people don't examine themselves to know why certain theories are interesting while others aren't. People don't normally discern their own motivations. Personally, I believe this is one of the most important things we can do as a follower of Jesus Christ. Scripture tells us the heart is "deceitful above all things." We simply cannot trust our own emotions, feelings, or perceptions of things. Therefore, we should be relying on facts rather than emotion. Instead of how a theory makes us feel, we should see if it holds up to scrutiny against fact-based information.

At the crux of many theories that seem to cause division in the Church is the personal feeling of possessing secret and special knowledge. There are many examples of this stem ming back to ancient gnosticism and even earlier. It is a very human compulsion and not rooted in the basic teachings of Christianity. According to scripture, the God of the Bible gives truth freely to all who seek it and are willing to learn. It is usually the people who are stubborn and set in their ways who remain ignorant to the truth, such as the Pharisees in Jesus' day. Conversely, the people who are too open to new ideas and are void of discernment also remain ignorant to the truth, such as the Gnostics from around the same time period. The trick is to be right in the middle; open to hearing out ideas yet discerning enough to know how to test them against scripture.

It is easy for a new and interesting idea to appeal to our pride as human beings. Most of us would feel special, perhaps even a sense of superiority, if we knew something about reality that most people do not. There are even those throughout time who have let the Gospel itself become an engine for personal pride. However, according to scripture, we are to put love above all else. We are to share truth, lovingly and patiently, while also realizing we are not going to have all the answers. We need to be able to identify the difference between the truth and our personal interpretation of truth' between observation and interpretation. If we fail in these regards, we are in danger of dividing the body of Christ. We are in danger of becoming Divisionist Christians. Divisionist Christianity (dividing the Church based on differing opinions) is one step away from Cannibal Christianity (emotionally abusing each other to feed our own egos), which is one more step from all-out war between Christians. This is why we have to set emotions aside and rely on facts. We also have to be able to identify the difference between salvation and non-salvation matters.

Personally, I find myself in the realm of Bible prophecy. I have always found it interesting. I love it. However, what is most exciting to me is thinking about the different ways things can play out. What exactly is the mark of the beast? An RFID chip? A piece of transhumanist technology? A splice of nephilim genes? Something else entirely? No one can say for absolute sure, but we are given enough information to at least know what kinds of things to stay away from and to prepare for what is ahead. In the meantime, how should we as Christians be treating each other in light of differences in interpretation? Is properly identifying the mark of the beast a salvation issue?

Some would say yes. Personally, I would say not yet. It could become a salvation issue when it is fully implemented. However, for now, we are not there yet. We are allowed to have difference in opinions. What we are not allowed to do, however, is divide over these issues. The mark of the beast is only one of many, many examples that could be given. Where the extremists in these groups based on alternate interpretations of scripture fail is to remind each other love must come first. Paul, John, and other stated so emphatically all throughout the New Testament. Unfortunately, we live in a world where a group is identified by its extremists. Most often, the extremists are the minority, yet they have the loudest voice. The reason is because the majority of Christians are polite, wanting not to offend, and most times bow out of a conversation or even an entire topic altogether so as to not contribute to arguing and bickering. This, of course, gives 100% of the speaking floor to the extremists.

I have found myself in the politeness camp, and I do still believe we should be respectful and courteous to others. However, we need to correctly focus how we actually go about doing that. I don't think we can remain silent anymore. This doesn't mean we need to get into arguments, of course. We also should be very familiar with the block and delete commands throughout all of social media. However, I believe there is a good medium of engagement that could give us, the majority, our voice back while also allowing us to put love first. It is all based on facts.

Arguments are purely emotional. One person decides to become personally offended by another person's opposing view, so they attack on a personal level. This is usually done through a "get them before they can get me" attitude. I used to be like this, years ago. For me, it was based solely on my own pride and insecurity. I have to imagine it is the same for others who choose to behave this way. The best way to combat this is to present facts void of emotion. If there is any emotion present at all, it must be love. We must also realize we do not have a personal responsibility to convince someone of something or change someone's mind. We do have a responsibility to teach the truth, of course, but if another person doesn't agree, they are allowed to make that choice. This even goes with the preaching of the Gospel; if we preach Jesus Christ to someone and they don't accept Him, that is their choice. We can pray for them and move on, but to try to force it on them would totally defeat the purpose.

We also need to learn how to remove people from our circles if they are not acting Christian or are sowing confusion and discord throughout our brethren. There is a time to disassociate. There is a time to remove the leaven. 99% of the time, this is due to a person's attitude; very rarely does it have to do with the person's actual beliefs. Just as a more modern example, I don't see anywhere in scripture that states it makes any difference if a person wants to believe the Earth is flat or a sphere. However, how that person acts based on his or her personal beliefs, that does matter. A lot. If a person is putting love first, the whole flat earth thing will come secondary to all the important things we should be focusing on as Christians. That person will understand his or her personal view is not the only one out there and that scripture can be interpreted in different ways to different people.

This brings us back to the fact that only 17 percent of Christians have an actual biblical worldview. The reason is because the internet and social media has provided us access to every view, opinion, feeling, emotion, thought, interpretation, and crazy idea in existence. More importantly, it is because Christians are finding it easy to accept anything they read because it feels right. It is easy to quote a Bible verse and let it support an original theory. Instead, we should be allowing the Bible to define our theories.

Anyone who knows me knows that quantum physics is an interest of mine. In fact, it is a great interest; a passion. Yet, it is by far not the most important thing for me to focus on as a Christian. Personally, I can read the Bible and see quantum physics all over it, as I have written and talked about many times before. However, I am no stranger to the idea that not everyone else will see scripture that way. Most people won't, in fact. This absolutely does not put me above anyone else. In fact, it is incredibly humbling as I am called to serve, therefore I feel it is my duty as a follower of Jesus Christ to put all of you above myself. This means, among many other things, thinking of ways to explain my line of thinking in a way anyone can understand, but also allowing people the right to disagree with me without allowing myself to contribute to unnecessary division. People are free to disagree. That does not afford me the right to be unloving and disrespectful, even if someone is rude to me first. The same goes for all Christians.

As important as quantum physics is to me personally, learning to love is far more important and needed in the Church, now more than ever. I feel a real calling to talk, write, and teach principles of love, even in light of our current social media culture. Facebook and YouTube do not exempt us from the basic, foundational principles of what it means to be a Christian. We are still required to love each other and love God, not either/or. We are still required to be servants to one another, not force others to serve our own egos by bullying them into agreeing with us. We are still required to be God's imagers across the Earth, regardless what shape it is or how we feel about it. The enemy has infiltrated our defenses. It is time for us to band together, reclaim our territory, and love one another even more than our own lives.

About the Author

Josh Peck works in full-time ministry at Prophecy Watchers. Josh is a documentary filmmaker and wrote, directed, and edited the blockbuster film *Silent Cry: The Darker Side of Trafficking*, along with *The Great Delusion: The Second Coming of Earth's Oldest Enemy* and *Ragnarok: Humanity's Last Stand*, all produced by SkyWatch Films, which Dr. Thomas Horn operated before his passing in 2023.

Josh is also the author of numerous bestselling books, including *The Lost Prophecies of Qumran: 2025 and the Final Age of Man*, *Afterlife* (coauthored with Donna Howell and Allie Anderson-Henson), *The Second Coming of the New Age* (coauthored with Steven Bancarz), *The Day The Earth Stands Still* (coauthored with Derek P. Gilbert), *Unraveling the*

Multiverse, and *Abaddon Ascending* (coauthored with bestselling author Tom Horn).

Josh is the founder and president of Daily Renegade (www.DailyRenegade.com) where he has hosted a variety of shows and podcasts. He has also been featured on numerous television and radio shows, including The Science Channel's *Forbidden History*, The History Channel's *In Search Of* with Zachary Quinto, *Coast to Coast AM* with George Noory, *Caravan to Midnight* with John B. Wells, and *The Hagmann Report* with Doug Hagmann. Josh is married to Christina Peck, with whom he has five children.

More from the Author

If you would like to find more books by Josh Peck, the best place to go is ProphecyWatchers.com where you will find these books as well as many more to come:

Is there a way for science and religion to complement one another? Does quantum physics have any place in the Bible? Do biblical interpretations have any use in explaining scientific observations? Is quantum physics unknowable to religious minds? Must a scientific mind also be void of religion? Is there an unseen world that exists all around us? Do things like strings, branes, multiple dimensions, parallel universes, time warps, quantum entanglement, and extradimensional beings have any place in biblical descriptions of God's creation? These questions and more are addressed in Quantum Creation. For the first time ever, the study of quantum physics is made available to the religious mind while explaining theological implications. Even better yet, the information is presented in a way anybody can understand. Learn just how perfectly compatible science and religion can be and why it seems they are always at odds. Discover what really makes up everything in existence as reality itself is examined at a quantum level. Find out if things like time travel are scientifically and biblically possible. What is presented in Quantum Creation is the answer to how science and religion really can go hand in hand. Finally, a way to look at the strange and fascinating world of quantum physics from

a biblical perspective is here. Includes Interviews with: Kenneth Johnson - Original Creator of V and Alien Nation, Dr. Ronald Mallett - Professor and Theoretical Physicist, and Dr. Ken Johnson - Biblical Researcher and Author

For years, the extraterrestrial hypothesis has dominated the field of ufology. However, there is another theory that might provide more substantial answers to the UFO phenomenon. In Cherubim Chariots, researcher and author Josh Peck explores the fringe of the extra-dimensional hypothesis to show the stunning possibility that UFOs and their pilots originate from a higher dimension. Discover answers to paradigm-shifting questions, such as:

* Were extra-dimensional craft and other-worldly beings reported in antiquity?

* Who are the mysterious cherubim and what is their role in the affairs of mankind?

* Did nonhuman entities leave behind evidence showing their extra-dimensional nature?

* Are higher dimensions interacting with our own?

* Are there prophecies pointing to a possible return of extra-dimensional beings?

* What is our true origin?

* How do we prepare for what is ahead?

... and much more! Cherubim Chariots - the definitive guide to extra-dimensional intelligences is here at last!

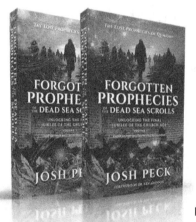

According to ancient texts that contain completely accurate prophecies to date, we are on the precipice of entering the final jubilee of the Church Age.

Who could have known how much influence the writings of a mysterious group of prophets and scribes hundreds of years before Christ would have on our understanding of end-times prophecy? As it turns out, much of what we've been taught about Israel in the First Century is incomplete. There were, in fact, Jewish believers who knew exactly what to expect in His first coming: that He would be God in the flesh and would die for our sins. If they accurately predicted the first arrival of Jesus, what did they say about His soon return?

In this groundbreaking updated and expanded two-volume edition of The Lost Prophecies of Qumran, you will learn:

- How an ancient Jewish/Essene calendar actually predicts the final year of mankind as we know it
- How the enigmatic group, known as the Essenes, was formed and what influence they had over the New Testament
- Lost prophecies only recently discovered in the Dead Sea Scrolls about our time today
- What messages the Essenes left behind for believers living in this present age
- How the prophecies of Daniel and Revelation fit within the ancient Essene prophetic calendar
- What hidden feasts and festivals the Essenes observed and what they point to in the future
- What were the circumstances of the disappearance of the Essenes and how it connects to every Christian from the past two thousand years

Once you learn about the Essenes and the Dead Sea Scrolls they left behind, you will understand the entirety of the Bible in a brand new light. Finally, the prophetic texts of Scripture can be understood as originally intended. Discover what God is revealing in these final years of our current age and what is ahead in the next age, soon to come!

Includes interviews with Dr. Ken Johnson, Dr. Judd Burton, Mondo Gonzales, Derek Gilbert, and Jim Barfield

Made in the USA
Monee, IL
09 April 2025

15502498R00118